About The Authors

G. Heinz and H. Donnay are two Belgian professors who were in Leopoldville and Elizabethville, respectively, and were close to the respective governments, in 1960 and 1961. Because of the nature of this book and the difficulties encountered in gathering information, and because they are both still involved in the economic and political fortunes of the Congo, the authors' identities had to be protected by pseudonyms.

At an MNC meeting in Leopoldville in 1959. Lumumba is speaking to the crowd, with Joseph Ileo at his left and Joseph Mobutu facing the camera on the extreme left.

— *Spécial*

A historic meeting in Kalamu at the end of December, 1958, when Lumumba returned from a trip to Accra. From left to right: Lumumba, Mongali, Njuvulu, and Ngalula. —*Spécial*

Even before independence, Lumumba was in contact with the PSA cadres in Kwilu. Here we see him being welcomed in Kikwit Cleophas Kamitatu in March, 1960.

—*Associated Press (Wide World Photos)*

LUMUMBA
The Last Fifty Days

By G. Heinz and H. Donnay
translated from the French by Jane Clark Seitz

Grove Press, Inc., New York

This translation copyright © 1969 by Grove Press, Inc.

All Rights Reserved

Originally published in French as
*Patrice Lumumba: Les cinquante derniers
jours de sa vie*, by Editions du C.R.I.S.P.
(Centre de Recherche et D'Information
Socio-Politiques), Brussels, and Editions
Le Seuil, Paris, copyright © 1966 by
Editions du C.R.I.S.P.

The section entitled "Patrice Lumumba Speaks"
was translated by Helen R. Lane.

No part of this book may be reproduced for any reason, by any
means, including any method of photographic reproduction, without
the permission of the publisher.

Library of Congress Catalog Card Number: 70-99428

First Evergreen Black Cat Edition, 1970

First Printing

Manufactured in the United States of America

". . . Everything possible was done to break my spirit, but I knew that in every country in the world freedom is the ideal for which all men in all times have fought and died. Having made a choice, that of serving my country . . . I was jeered at, vilified, dragged in the mud—simply because I insisted on freedom for our country. I have never been against whites, I have never been against people, but what I have always rebelled against was injustice. . . ."

PATRICE LUMUMBA, FROM A SPEECH TO THE
"AMIS DE *Présence Africaine*," 1960.

Contents

Preface

On January 17, 1961, two hundred days after the declaration of independence of the Congo, Patrice Lumumba was struck down by violent death in Elizabethville.

Founder of the Mouvement National Congolais (MNC —National Congolese Movement) in October, 1958, it was he who, in June, 1960, at the end of the Belgian colonial regime, had formed the first sovereign government of the Republic of the Congo. Within a few weeks, he was to experience an outbreak of violence by the ex-Force Publique (Public Force—Congolese colonial army), Belgian military intervention, the secession of Katanga and South Kasai, the action of the *casques bleus*[1] of the UN, tribal wars in Kasai, a brutal rupture in his alliance with President Kasavubu, the military coup d'état of Colonel Mobutu, his house arrest in Leopoldville, imprisonment in Thysville, and threats of death.

Alive, Lumumba was a personality who aroused all kinds of contradictory reactions.

Dead, Lumumba continues to weigh heavily on the life and destiny of the Congo and of Africa. It is in his name that groups and countries confront one another;

[1] These were soldiers belonging to a UN force sent to the Congo in 1960, identified as *casques bleus* because of the blue helmets they wore.—*Translator's note.*

ix

it is in the name of fidelity to his mission that the masses are rebelling, armed against established power, for he is the focus of a myth whose force goes beyond his life as a man.

However, the death of Lumumba himself still remains a mystery in many respects. Little is known of the conditions surrounding his death, and the most contradictory versions have been circulated, sometimes with the goal of destroying adversaries and discrediting the politics they represent.

The UN has not been able to clarify certain decisive aspects of this tragic fate: some witnesses have disappeared; some sources are inaccessible.

Nonetheless it is essential for the political future of the Congo that the entire truth one day be revealed about the death of Lumumba, the context in which it took place, the mechanisms which determined the event, and the principal actors whose responsibility it was.

It is not our task here to carry out a police investigation, especially as we have neither the means nor the power. We have, nonetheless, carried out a detailed political investigation. We have tried to preserve a descriptive character in the work, clarifying the facts without putting anyone on trial. Often, in order not to compromise the security of the people mentioned, we have not revealed any names, publication of which is not essential for an understanding of the facts. We have also tried to place the events in the perspective of the emotional climate of the time and, through the text and the pictures, to establish an authenticity which permits us to have a living approach to an elusive truth.

Our inquiry demanded a great deal of research and many interviews in Belgium, the Congo, and other countries. We have not found all that we had hoped to find. In addition, many clues have been lost forever. Nonetheless, our patient and objective research has permitted us to close in on the real facts, to discard false information, and to eliminate biased interpretations and polemics.

The frame of our narration is firm; it is within this frame that the truth is inscribed, all the truth that one day will perhaps be fully revealed.

G. H. and H. D.

LUMUMBA

The Last Fifty Days

Photo taken in June, 1960, when Kasavubu and Lumumba had decided to cooperate. Cyrille Adoula (in middle) encouraged this reconciliation. —Associated Press (Wide World Photos)

Maurice Mpolo (at left) in July, 1960, in his job as Colonel of the ANC. —Congopresse

PART 1
"The Big Rabbit Has Escaped"

Lumumba among the people of the Cité in Leopoldville on October 9, 1960. ——*Associated Press (Wide World Photos)*

Photo taken in July, 1960, after the Belgian military intervention, when Kasavubu and Lumumba were "like the fingers of a hand."
——*Associated Press (Wide World Photos)*

Also on October 9, 1960, Lumumba speaking at a friend's house.
——*UPI (Jarland)*

The Departure

A heavy tropical rain had been falling since 9 o'clock on the Sunday evening of November 27, 1960. At the Tilkens residence in Leopoldville-Kalina, the Congolese prime minister, Patrice Lumumba,* was preparing for his clandestine departure to Stanleyville, his loyal city.[1] There he hoped to meet the national president of the PSA (Parti Solidaire Africain—African Party of Solidarity), Antoine Gizenga,* who had seized power in mid-November in the name of the first Congolese central government.

Around the house were several cordons of troops. The closest one was made up of UN *casques bleus,* a large number of them Ghanaians, who were guarding the Congolese leader and patroling the entrances to the house. Outside the UN cordon were Congolese soldiers, belonging to the ANC (Armée Nationale Congolaise—Congolese National Army) of young Colonel Mobutu,* officially loyal to the Board of Commissioners General.

It was this Board, presided over by Justin Bomboko,* ex-Minister of Foreign Affairs, that held power at that moment in Leopoldville.

The role of the Congolese soldiers was to prevent Lumumba from leaving his home, as he had previously

[1] Africans discussed in this book whose names have an asterisk beside them are described in greater detail at the end of the volume in a Biographical Note.

3

done, in order to speak to his faithful followers in the
Cité.[2] The soldiers were under orders to arrest him immediately if he made the least attempt to leave. The ANC
—represented by paratroopers stationed in the street and
by a second group near the building that now is the Cour
des Comptes (Audit Office)—was to check all those who
entered the building and all who left, because the government wanted to isolate Lumumba and separate him from
his friends on the outside. In fact, the ANC was for the
most part only interested in checking identities, but from
time to time it forbade servants to leave the residence
to go to market and Lumumba's children to go to school.

The rain and the storm had reduced the guard on that
November 27. The UN guards, as well as ANC soldiers,
took refuge in a small building. The big Chevrolet stationwagon of the MNC—driven by Lumumba's chauffeur—
left the grounds. The first Congolese guards were led to
believe that, as usual, the Chevrolet held Lumumba's
brother, Louis, or else the servants, who were on their
way back to their homes in the *Cité*. The UN guards did
not appear; they were not in charge of watching the exits
and besides, a few moments before, Lumumba had been
seen inside the house.

Patrice Lumumba, the man whom Victor Nendaka* of
the Congolese Sûreté[3] referred to in code as "the big
rabbit," was in the car, crouched behind the front seat.
The boys, seated behind, covered him as well as possible.
The paracommandos were more vigilant; they stopped
the Chevrolet and prepared to search it. The chauffeur
told them in a very natural voice that he was going to

---

[2] The *Cité*, a French colonial term, is that section of a city where
most of the so-called "natives" live.—*Translator's note*.

[3] The Congolese security agency, similar to the FBI.

buy cigarettes and would be right back. The paracommandos let the car through . . . the car sped toward the Guinean Embassy where Lumumba was to meet his wife Pauline and his son Roland, who were at this time living at a cousin's house in Leopoldville.

This is the true story of Lumumba's departure for Stanleyville. Other versions exist, some of them quite close to the truth. Some say that the departure took place earlier, between 6 and 7 o'clock, but do not explain what happened before midnight. Another version has circulated in European circles in Leopoldville, based on the impressions of J. Cordy, a Belgian journalist and correspondent of *Le Soir;* he was at his brother's house on Avenue Tilkens during the evening of November 27. He heard a motorboat going up the river and deduced that the escape took place at that time by boat.

In Katanga, during secession, the news of Lumumba's dismissal is received with enthusiasm.
    —*Associated Press*
    (Wide World Photos)

In mid-September, 1960, Col. Mobutu announced that he was "neutralizing" all the political leaders.
    —*Jeune Afrique (Dalmas)*

African CASQUES BLEUS *guard Lumumba's house during October and November, 1960.*   —*Belga*

Face to face during the most tense period of 1960, a detachment of CASQUES BLEUS *(at left) and the* ANC *in Leopoldville.* —*Congopresse*

Toward Stanleyville?

For Patrice Lumumba, the days preceding November 27 were particularly tense.

For the past few days, under orders from Lumumba, the leaders of the MNC, the PSA, Céréa, and other parties favorable to the prime minister, had been trying to get to Stanleyville by traveling through Kwilu. Each one carried a letter of introduction to the provincial president of Leopoldville Province, Cléophas Kamitatu,* one of the leaders of the PSA, as well as an itinerary drawn up and recommended by him. Among these men were Ministers Gbenye,* Mbuyi,* Kashamura,* Massena,* Mulele,* President of the Senate Joseph Okito,* and some elected members of parliament of Lumumbist sympathy, such as Mr. Bocheley-Davidson,* Mr. Rudahindwa,* Gabriel Yumbu,* and Georges Grenfell.*

The itineraries were all different so as to reduce the risks involved. The local PSA sections were invited to aid the fugitives, but it was recommended that Lumumba himself avoid the town of Kikwit where, on November 26, Pierre Mulele and Gabriel Yumbu had held a public meeting. Colonel Mobutu had in fact sent commandos there on the morning of the twenty-seventh; they were sent to prevent a mutiny among the local military police, to disarm them and protect the Mukongo minority against eventual attacks by the PSA population. This affair resulted, nonetheless, in the deaths of dozens of people.

At that moment, plans for the departure of Lumumba had not even been revealed to his close associates. The original plan of the MNC leader had been to group his partisans and collaborators in Stanleyville while he himself would stay on in Leopoldville. From Stanleyville, a position of strength, the Lumumbists would then exert vigorous pressure for his liberation. But a new factor caused Lumumba to modify his plan. Ten days earlier, the man who brought Lumumba his mail and established all liaison with the outside world, Antoine-Roger Bolamba,* brought him an eight-page document drawn up by a member of the cabinet of the prime minister. This document was a plea in favor of the institution of a Lumumbist power in Stanleyville; the ANC in the interior, said the document, was, on the whole, quite pro-Lumumba and an attack against Leopoldville from Kenge in Kwilu and from Bolobo on the river would have every chance of succeeding. In the economic and financial domain, a blockade of Leopoldville—backed up by the creation of a currency which would be accepted in the whole country, except for Katanga and Leopoldville—would cause economic chaos. Finally, in the psychological domain, propaganda spread by Patrice Lumumba on Radio Stanleyville would be a fearful weapon against his adversaries. This plan was based on the hypothesis that the UN force, which would inevitably be activated during the Lumumbist offensive, would show its good will by remaining neutral.

This plan to regroup in Stanleyville convinced Lumumba. Three days after the transmission of the plan, its author was able to come to the Congolese prime minister's house, in spite of the difficulties presented by the

ANC surveillance.[4] Lumumba then gave to him, under seal of secrecy, a written note addressed to the ambassadors from Guinea and the United Arab Republic in Leopoldville: he wanted to obtain from these countries a helicopter, or some kind of air transportation, which would be available near Leopoldville at the right time. It seems that neither Sekou Touré nor Nasser had any knowledge of this request.

It was then that Patrice Lumumba looked for another method. The presence of his brother and the frequent use of the Chevrolet stationwagon belonging to the MNC would create a certain confusion in the minds of the Congolese soldiers charged with his surveillance. The choice of November 27—the day of the triumphal return of President Kasavubu* to Leopoldville from the United States—is largely explained by the conviction that this day would be marked by a certain lack of vigilance.

To prepare for his departure, a member of Patrice Lumumba's cabinet, Bernardin Diaka,* was asked to explore the route, that is the road toward Kenge in Kwilu. On November 23, he scouted the route: the road was not blocked; ferries would assure a normal crossing of the rivers, and there was, some 55 miles from Leopoldville, a small emergency Air-Brousse air field. A report of these findings was made to the ambassadors of Guinea and the U.A.R. as well as to Patrice Lumumba.

In preparation for his departure, Lumumba issued a check for 50,000 Congolese francs; it was collected from Socobanque by Bernardin Diaka.

---

[4] A lot depended on the mood of the guards. Sometimes, when he was waiting for visitors, Patrice Lumumba came to greet them himself in the street. The men in charge of guarding him still retained a certain amount of respect for their ex-leader, and he even had some measure of authority over them.

On the morning of the twenty-seventh, the representatives of two African countries were informed of the plan for departure; the Congolese prime minister would not accept financial assistance or even the car offered by the Guinean ambassador. He turned, instead, to Cleophas Kamitatu, through the intermediary of UN officers, at 9 A.M. He asked Kamitatu to put his family car at his disposal; it was a blue Peugeot, new, but already broken in.

Kamitatu was worried. Why act so quickly, without, he believed, real preparation? He was not the only one who was frightened, as this statement by Thomas Kanza* demonstrates:

I was one of the privileged people who could exchange words with the deceased [Lumumba], before his flight to Stanleyville. I had a chance to speak with him for two hours on the telephone. In the course of our conversation, I did my best to convince him not to leave his house guarded by Ghanaians and to wait, even indefinitely, for the resolution of the Congolese crisis. The flight amounted to suicide. No, he replied, it will be difficult for you to realize that one of us must die to save the cause of our homeland.[5]

The same day, Minister Alexander Mahamba,* as well as the mayor of Leopoldville, the Mukongo Daniel Kanza,* father of Thomas, both tried to dissuade him. But Lumumba had made up his mind. He gave instructions to his friends in Kwilu who would be in charge of the flight toward Orientale Province.

President Kamitatu contacted the control tower in Kikwit from Ndjili, and in the afternoon the commissioners of police of Kenge and Kikwit called him by shortwave. The first arrangements were made to wel-

[5] *Le Martyr*, newspaper published in Stanleyville, October 12 and 13, 1964.

come and help the fugitives during their transit through Kwilu. On the other hand, Joseph Kasongo,* president of the Chamber, who was invited to join Lumumba, did not believe it possible to take the risk, despite the formal offer transmitted to him by special messenger.

On leaving his house, Patrice Lumumba went to the Guinean Embassy. His wife Pauline was not there for their rendezvous; he sent his chauffeur in the Chevrolet into Leopoldville and he himself left the embassy in the Peugeot, driven by Diaka and escorted by a Mutetela commander, while a Guinean captain went along with them, also in a Peugeot. When they reached the Astoria, the Guinean officer took Patrice Lumumba in his car, because, according to him, Diaka was going too slowly. He planned to leave Lumumba just after he crossed the Nsele River, beyond Ndjili. At that point only Diaka was armed, because the Congolese prime minister had left his .22 long rifle in the Chevrolet.

Diaka's Peugeot was slowed down by an incident just after crossing the Nsele in the Minkawa Valley. The Chevrolet carrying Pauline and Roland caught up with him, and Lumumba climbed into the car. Diaka stopped to change a tire and subsequently got lost and bogged down in the mud before he arrived at the Kwango ferry around 4 o'clock in the morning. A Fiat was waiting there with Louis Akunda,* ex-chief of the cabinet of Minister Mpolo, and Victor Wungudi, administrative secretary to Patrice Lumumba, both Batetela. They had left Leopoldville the morning of the twenty-seventh.

The Kwango boat stayed on the other side of the river. Since the Batetela did not speak the language of Kwilu they had not been able to convince either the fishermen or the boatmen to take them across.

Diaka crossed the river in a canoe, armed with a .22

long rifle, and succeeded in arranging for the crossing of
the three cars. Lumumba gave 5,000 francs and a twenty-
four-hour vacation to the boatmen. This incident at the
ferry was apparently due to a delay on the part of the
fugitives.[6] A functionary from Kwilu, assisted by the
police, was supposed to have taken charge of them and
report to Kamitatu. According to a very simple code, ap-
plied between Leopoldville on the one hand and Kikwit
and Kenge on the other, Lumumba was "the package" or
"the big brother"; Kamitatu was "300"; Kikwit was
"Diba" and Kenge was "Iks."

While the fugitives were trying to reach the Kwango
ferry, President Kasavubu, having returned from New
York via Paris, was holding a reception in his palace.
All the authorities, both civil and military, were celebrating the victory of the chief of state in the United
Nations in his political conflict with Lumumba: the recognition of his delegation by the General Assembly and,
therefore, the disavowal of the Lumumbist delegation.
This fact, it has often been said, would explain why the
departures to Stanleyville were so precipitous; because
of the vote in the UN and despite the reassuring statements by Kasavubu that the next Round Table would be
open to all, the Lumumbists were led to believe that UN
protection would be refused them, and thus the arrest of
their principal leaders could take place. We have seen
above that this was not the only reason, and perhaps not
even the principal motivation, for departure.

[6] The use of the word "fugitives" does not imply any pejorative
judgment of the actions of Patrice Lumumba and his friends.

A Prime Minister in a
Guarded Residence

How was it possible, a mere five months after the independence festivities, for a situation to develop which caused the prime minister to leave the capital in secret to go to Stanleyville?

Patrice Lumumba's fate was really sealed on September 5, 1960. At 8:10 A.M., the English lesson on the radio was interrupted and President Kasavubu declared over the microphone:

I have a most important piece of news to announce. The Prime Mayor,[7] who was named by the King of the Belgians . . . has betrayed the mission that was assigned him. . . . He has governed arbitrarily . . . and even now he is in the midst of throwing the country into an atrocious civil war. That is why I have decided I should immediately dissolve the government. . . .

That evening, Patrice Lumumba gave his answer before the same microphone:

The popular government will remain in power. I proclaim that, as of today, Kasavubu, who has betrayed the nation, who has betrayed the people by collaborating

[7] He was, of course, speaking of the Prime Minister.—*Editor's note.*

with the Belgians and the Flemish, is no longer the Chief
of State.

Thus the rupture between the two Congolese leaders
came about—the two leaders chosen by the new parliamentary assemblies on the eve of independence in June,
1960, to hold the two highest offices in the new state:
Joseph Kasavubu, President of the Republic, elected by
an overwhelming majority (159 to 43, with 11 absten-
tions) and Patrice Lumumba, head of the first government in which all parties were represented, except for
the MNC–Kalonji branch, a party which was essentially
composed of Baluba of Kasai and to which President of
the Senate Joseph Ileo* belonged.

President and founder of the party that was, nu-
merically, the best represented in the Chamber, the recognized leader of a large coalition of nationalist parties
with positions of strength in Orientale Province, Kivu,
Kwilu, North Katanga, and Kasai, Patrice Lumumba was
able to effect a national union (more apparent than
real) and to integrate the Bas-Congo into his government. He had thus isolated the confederalists of the Conakat, whose last attempts at secession before June 30,
1960 had failed because of the combined actions of the
central Congolese authorities and the Belgian minister
Ganshof van der Meersch.[8]

When trouble broke out in early July in the Force
Publique in Leopoldville, in Thysville, then in Elizabethville, and finally in a chain reaction throughout the whole
country, the Congolese noncommissioned officers and soldiers demanded the immediate appointment of black officers and the dismissal of the commander in chief,

---

[8] For the political events of this era, see the work of J. Gérard-
Libois and Benoît Verhaegen: *Congo 1960*, volume 2, and a supple-
ment published by Dossiers du C.R.I.S.P., Brussels, 1961.

General Janssens. When, with the help of Belgian military intervention, Moise Tshombe* had proclaimed the independence of Katanga on July 11, 1960, and when a Belgian military operation against Matadi had accelerated the rupture between Leopoldville and Brussels, the two Congolese political chiefs, President Kasavubu and Prime Minister Lumumba, acted in perfect accord, going together to Luluabourg, Kindu, and Elizabethville (where the provincial minister of the interior had refused them permission to land), then later to Stanleyville.

It was again in concert on July 14 that Lumumba and Kasavubu launched, in Kindu, an appeal to the U.S.S.R. and announced the breaking of relations with Belgium. Together they asked for military intervention by the UN on the twelfth and thirteenth to oust the Belgian forces who were based at Kamina and to put an end to the Katangese secession.

All this caused Lumumba to say on July 22, on Radio Leopoldville:

Between the Chief of State and me there is a unity of view, a unity of logic, a solidarity and not one needle can come between this friendship. . . . This unity between the Chief of State and me is what makes the independent Congo strong.

Beyond appearances and their actions in common in July, 1960, a profound difference rapidly separated the chief of state and the prime minister during the month of August. In fact, Patrice Lumumba, having lost patience, complained openly to the secretary general of the UN, accusing him [Kasavubu] of making deals directly with the secessionists and deliberately ignoring the central authorities; at that moment he was contemplating using

force against Kasai and Katanga; he had taken exceptional measures against the project for a State of Central
Congo (which was envisaged by certain Abakists) and
other exceptional measures to neutralize the opposition
which, from all sides, was mounting against Lumumba
in Leopoldville.

The desire to overthrow Lumumba and the fear of being eliminated by him formed a common denominator
between his opponents. The confederalist Abakists, sus-
tained by French agents (such as Delarue and Jayle),
in the service of Abbé Youlou, said (on August 21, 1960)
through Vital Moanda,* President of the province of Central Congo, that it was their intention to "rid the Congo
of Patrice Lumumba by legal or illegal means."

The Kalonjists were embittered and had not forgiven
Lumumba for having eliminated their leader from the
central government; they wanted to have leaders in Leopoldville who would look with favor upon their province
or state, South Kasai (the mining state of Bakwanga),
which was more or less secessionist; Joseph Ngalula*
and Albert Kalonji* were organizing the Luba tribe with
this in mind.

Catholics, backed by the local bishop, Monseigneur
Malula, and by the Christian-Democratic press, such as
the *Courrier d'Afrique* (suspended on August 20) and
Présence Congolaise (which stopped printing in August),
denounced the Lumumbist arguments as Communist- or
crypto-Soviet-inspired slogans.

The syndicalists of the Union des Travailleurs Con-
golais (UTC—Union of Congolese Workers) and of the
Fédération Générale du Travail du Kongo (FGTK—
General Federation of Labor of the Congo) and of the
Association du Personnel Indigene de la Colonie (APIC

—Association of Native Workers of the Colony) accused the political authorities of demagoguery, tribalism, corruption, inefficiency, and powerlessness when confronted with growing unemployment and inflation.

The Ngombe (Bangala) of the Parti de l'Unité Nationale (PUNA—Party of National Unity) had seen their leader, Jean Bolikango,* arrested for involvement in a plot after having publicly taken a position in favor of the return of foreign and Belgian technicians. The young branch of the party—the Jepuna—had mandated delegates in Katanga in secession and openly approved of Moise Tshombe.

These different opposition groups had members at the heart of the government, with Delvaux* and Bomboko in the Senate, as well as Ileo, Adoula,* and the lawyer Promontorio, or in the ministerial cabinet, with technicians such as Kandolo* in the prime minister's office, Ndele* in Finance, and Mbeka* in Planning. They also had favorable elements in the National Army (ANC), notably among the Baluba, the Ngombe, and the Bakongo.

Exterior influences simultaneously played a part. In Abbé Youlou's entourage in Brazzaville, the objective was to directly influence President Kasavubu, who was sent, with this goal in mind, several private counselors before June, 1960—among them the lawyer Croquez from Paris and the Belgian Dehalu. Some Belgian "antennas," private or official, were also quite active, especially after the expulsion from Leopoldville, on August 10, of Ambassador van den Bosch. These men had money and the means for propaganda, both written and by radio, at their disposal.

We must realize that, even before June 30, Patrice Lumumba was considered in European circles—political, religious, and business—as a Congolese politician who must be kept from power; certain among them violently expressed their hostility. Thus the Belgian journalist, Pierre De Vos, reported that a Belgian director of some important colonial companies hoped, on the eve of independence, to see Lumumba liquidated by "a bullet through his head. . . . I would be pleased to discover, in one of the insane asylums in Kasai, a madman who would carry out this work."

The speech delivered on June 30 to the Chamber by Patrice Lumumba in the presence of King Baudouin, denouncing the Belgian colonial system, gained for him a certain renewed hostility in European circles in the Congo, and in Belgium, and this was to contribute, during the troubles within the Force Publique at the beginning of July, to the Belgian version of events that saw him as the man most responsible for the violence and cruelty.

From this moment on, the conservative Belgian press did not hesitate to attack Lumumba directly and even to say that his death would be a blessing for the Congo and for the Belgians living in the Congo. Thus, in the issue of July 12, 1960, *La Libre Belgique,* a conservative Catholic daily, stated that several Lumumbist ministers "acted like primitive savages and imbeciles or like Communist creatures." In the same paper, on July 27, 1960, Marcel de Corte, professor of ethics and philosophy at the University of Liège, attacked Lumumba more directly: "He is a barbarian, who causes the officers to weep with rage, officers who with a single gesture could have rid the planet of his bloody effrontery."

At the beginning of September the tension between the chief of the government and his opponents grew. Soviet planes were seen in Stanleyville and Czech technicians in Leopoldville; the first news of massacres in

South Kasai, carried out by elements of the ANC, was reaching the city; unverifiable rumors about an imminent Lumumbist coup d'état were being spread; it was said that an ANC offensive was about to be launched against North Katanga, and the relations between Mr. Hammarskjöld, Secretary General of the UN, and the Lumumba –Gizenga–Kashamura group were getting worse and worse because of the UN Council's refusal to furnish the means of fighting the Katangese secession by force.

It was in this atmosphere, after a mid-August, 1960, appeal by Kasavubu for unity and respect for legally established authorities, and after the Pan-African Conference of Ministers in Leopoldville where Lumumba received rather substantial support, that the break between Kasavubu and Lumumba suddenly took place on September 5. For some ten days total confusion reigned. On September 13, Lumumba obtained a majority (later contested) in Parliament, granting him the full powers that he had demanded. But because the UN had decided to neutralize the airports and the radio throughout the territory, Lumumba was placed in the impossible position of attempting to impose his authority effectively in Leopoldville, where his armed guard of one hundred men would hardly suffice. Joseph Ileo, the leader chosen by Kasavubu, was not able to form a government capable of influencing Parliament or exercising effective authority in spite of the support furnished by Radio Congo of Brazzaville and some of the foreign diplomatic corps.

On September 10, 1960, the Belgian Minister of Foreign Affairs made it clear to his representative at Brazzaville that the "constituted authorities have the duty of putting Lumumba in a position where he cannot cause trouble."

On September 14 at 8:30 P.M., Colonel Mobutu, chief

staff officer of the ANC and former Secretary of State personally promoted by Patrice Lumumba, ordered the "neutralization" of all political institutions, further forbidding the chief of state, the Parliament, and the Ileo and Lumumba governments to undertake or initiate any action, and granting the Board of Commissioners General the right to exercise all power. This measure greatly damaged the position of Lumumba and his friends because, on September 29, the Board of Commissioners, without consulting Colonel Mobutu, declared itself responsible to Chief of State Kasavubu. Furthermore, its President, Justin Bomboko, and several commissioners, among them the most important (Mbeka, Ndele, Cardoso,* Kazadi,* and Nussbaumer,* for example), had been recruited from among Lumumba's most relentless opponents.

Henceforth, Lumumba's fate became uncertain. As early as September 6, a warrant for the arrest of the Congolese prime minister was issued, signed by René Rom, attorney general of the Court of Appeals of Leopoldville, under orders from Joseph Ileo, "Prime Minister and Minister of Justice." Ileo's order contained the following formal charge, which was the basis for the warrant for the immediate arrest of Lumumba:

Leopoldville, September 6, 1960

His Honor, The Attorney General of the Court of Appeals of and at Leopoldville

Mr. Attorney General,
Herewith, I have the honor of ordering you to proceed with the immediate arrest of Patrice Lumumba, member of the House of Representatives, on the basis of the following charge:

After having been dismissed from his functions as Prime Minister on September 5, 1960, by an order of the Chief of State, countersigned by Ministers Albert Delvaux and Justin Bomboko, the aforementioned did from nine to ten P.M. on the same day give violent public speeches on the *Radiodiffusion Nationale Congolaise* [National Congolese Radio], inciting the population to overthrow the established authorities and the legal regime installed according to the Fundamental Law of May 19, 1960.

> (*signed*) The Prime Minister and Minister
> of Justice
> Joseph Ileo

The same day, René Rom sent a note to Lumumba asking that he come immediately to his office. A warrant of arrest was drawn up requesting "all members of the Force Publique to lend aid if necessary" in order that Patrice Lumumba, "charged with exciting the population against established authority," be arrested and brought before the public prosecutor. On September 14, René Rom was to admit to Rémy Mwamba,* minister of justice of the Lumumba government, that he had signed the letter and the document "under moral constraint" from the chief of state. He was apparently brought before Joseph Kasavubu at 10 A.M. by G. Denis, one of Kasavubu's European advisers, and was forced to stay there against his will until 12:20 A.M. the next day. This, in any case, is the story that emerged from the official administrative report of Minister Mwamba, the man who interrogated Rom.

The fourteenth day of the month of September in the year 1964; before us are Rémy Mwamba, Minister of Justice of the Republic of the Congo, and René Rom,

Attorney General of the Court of Appeals, to whom we
pose the following questions:

Q: Do you admit having signed on September 6, 1960,
a warrant for the arrest of the Prime Minister, Patrice
Lumumba?

A: Yes, under moral constraint.

Q: Under what circumstances did you sign the order?

A: Mr. Denis, in a car belonging to the chief of state,
came to get me at my office at 10 A.M.

Q: Did you take the warrant forms with you at that
time?

A: No.

Q: Where did you get this printed form?

A: Since I refused to draw up the warrant by hand,
the President ordered me to take his car and, accompanied by two Congolese whose names I did not know, to
go and get the warrant forms. Instead of taking the war-
rant-for-arrest forms, I instead took a summons form
with me.

On September 11, on the basis of this warrant, the
Bangala military police arrested Lumumba between 3
and 4 P.M. in his residence on Albert Boulevard (now the
Boulevard of June 30) and brought him to the military
camp. He was quickly freed. Lumumba maintained that
it was the faithful soldiers who released him, but the
ANC General Lundula* was probably the decisive factor.
(Later the same day the General was dismissed by President Kasavubu.) Liberated, Lumumba, with a military
escort of fifty men, went to the African sector of the city
(the *Cité*) and spoke to the crowds.

On Thursday, September 15, just after Colonel Mobutu, who was in contact with Western representatives,
had decreed the neutrality of the government and of the
political institutions, Lumumba tried to rally the military
to his side in Camp Leopold; but in fact he was in a

delicate position there. Baluba soldiers from Kasai, who accused him of being responsible for the massacres of the Bakwanga, menaced him: ". . . either he dies to-night or we will die." And the Congolese leader owed his life to the refuge he found in the officers' mess of the UN Ghanaian soldiers and also to the protection furnished by the UN soldiers who fought off his assailants. That evening, Patrice Lumumba was brought back to his residence by an ANC truck, which left the camp (under the protection of men loyal to Mobutu and the Ghanaian soldiers) despite vociferous comments and hostile cries from unarmed soldiers.

Lumumba, arrested again on September 16, managed to escape again; on the eighteenth he returned to his house. UN protection was organized by Mr. Rajeshwar Dayal, personal representative of the Secretary General; he had refused to accede to Ileo's and Kasavubu's demands that he arrest Lumumba. On September 21, the ANC guard of the house was lifted because of the Sudanese protection furnished to Lumumba. Several attempts were made to reconcile the differences between Kasavubu and Patrice Lumumba, at the initiation, and with the help, of a so-called "compromise" Commission[9] from the Parliament comprised of Okito, Kasongo, and Weregemere* and with the moral support of Colonel Mobutu. Several projects for Round Table discussions were outlined. These attempts failed, but by the end of September they had created a certain relaxation of tension. Some of Lumumba's ministers who had been arrested, among them Gizenga and Mpolo (named Lieutenant General on September 13 by Lumumba) were freed on September

[9] The Commission was ordered to encourage a compromise between Lumumba and Kasavubu.

24. The next day, Lumumba, escorted by his guard and African soldiers, was able to travel around the *Cité* by car. On October 1 he was even a dinner guest of the Guineans of the UN.

However, the time was not right for reconciliation.

In reply to President Nkrumah of Ghana—who affirmed that Colonel Mobutu's action was subversive, that Ileo's government was fraught with illegality, and furthermore that Kasavubu and Lumumba were the only legitimate authority in the Congo—the Congolese President stated in a telegram dated September 30, 1960:

You should learn the facts about the banditry and terrorism carried out under Lumumba's influence. You should learn the facts about the social chaos in the Congo —the large number of unemployed and of unhappy and pitiable people—brought about in two months' time by the foolhardy actions of Lumumba, and this in spite of my repeated warnings. You should learn the facts about the tens of thousands of Kasai men, women, and children who were massacred in the Congo.

Several commissioners general, some of them very important, were determined to obtain the arrest of Lumumba, but they ran into several obstacles: the attitude of the UN, administrative incoherence, Mobutu's behavior—in their eyes ambiguous,—and the ineffectualness of the ANC.

The Board of Commissioners General debated the problem on several occasions. The following passages are extracted from the minutes of the meeting of this Board:

Commissioner General of National Education Mario Cardoso said on September 24: "I have discovered that there are a great many different tribes in the army, so that they don't dare arrest Lumumba." Commissioner

General of the Interior José Nussbaumer added: "Colonel [Mobutu] is afraid of arresting people."

On September 26, Commissioner of Justice Etienne Tshisekedi* suggested that Lumumba's house be surrounded by soldiers of the ANC Army and that all who attempted to enter or exit therefrom be arrested. Later, after another member of the Board charged that Patrice Lumumba was bringing in agents from Stanleyville to assassinate the commissioners, Albert Ndele, Vice-President of the Board, decided, "on the advice of the Council, to have Lumumba's residence surrounded by two squads of Congolese soldiers." The next day the Board learned that Colonel Mobutu did not implement the decision. In the meantime a curious event involving the disappearance of a warrant for arrest took place. Commissioner Nussbaumer was kidnapped and molested by Lumumbists on September 27, and a week later the courts had not renewed the stolen warrant, which was necessary if measures were to be taken against Lumumba.

Colonel Mobutu's reticent attitude, the UN's lack of cooperation, and the affair of the unrenewed warrant all added to the discouragement among the members of the Board. The president of the sessions demonstrated this discouragement in a statement he made on October 4: ". . . as long as this rascal is free, there is no use working." "This rascal" was Patrice Lumumba, the man a commissioner called "an assassin whom we have made the mistake of letting free."

This climate reinforced the bitterness of the Board toward the UN and led it to take stronger action against Lumumba.

As early as the twenty-second, and then again on the twenty-ninth, Colonel Mobutu and President Kasavubu

demanded the withdrawal of Guinean and Ghanaian UN
contingents because of "their direct and conspicuous
support of Patrice Lumumba." Later, relations worsened,
especially after the publication of the Dayal Report on
the ANC, the Board of Commissioners, and the return
of the Belgians. The report was especially severe vis à
vis the Congolese soldiers and the de facto authority
established by Colonel Mobutu.

Beginning on October 10, the Congolese prime minister
could avoid the ANC only by not leaving his house and
with the constant protection of the UN guard. That day,
in fact, an attempt to arrest "Patrice Lumumba, deputy"
was made by some two hundred men, and failed because
of UN protection. Besides, at the last moment, the Congolese soldiers realized that Colonel Mobutu had not given
them the necessary warrant for arrest. The next day, the
house was encircled by the ANC.

At that time, following a new and spectacular "sortie"
by the Congolese prime minister on Sunday the ninth—
during which he gave several public speeches before
enthusiastic crowds—Justin Bomboko sent a veritable
ultimatum to the UN: "The ANC is ready to do battle
with the UN in order to arrest Patrice Lumumba."

Congolese armored trucks were called up from Camp
Thysville, and the guard was reinforced in order to eliminate the Lumumba partisans. But, finally, on October 12,
after bargaining with General Rickhye of the UN, Justin
Bomboko, as well as the Colonel, agreed to the following
formula: Patrice Lumumba would not be apprehended,
but instead would be transferred to a more secluded
residence and deprived of political power. In fact, nothing
was done in this regard, essentially because the Colonel
refused to give his endorsement to a show of force

against the house. "If Patrice Lumumba comes out, the guard will arrest him," he said on October 13. That was all. It was not the task of "neutral" President Kasavubu to give the order for anyone's arrest nor was it Bomboko's job to give such orders to the ANC. The arrest warrant remained valid, but he, Mobutu, would only authorize use of it if Patrice Lumumba attempted to escape in order to carry on his political activity.

Issued on the night of a Lumumbist attempt against Ndele, this Mobutu formula did not please the Board when, on October 15, it was proposed "to proceed with the systematic isolation of Lumumba and with the arrest of all his clique." Furthermore, it was suggested that "the electricity and water in his house be cut off," while at the same time Gilbert Pongo,* agent of the Sûreté, demanded a "thorough purge of every Lumumbist element."[10] There was, however, a fault in this plan: "I have no intention of letting my soldiers be killed for Lumumba," the Colonel declared on October 17, upon his return from Elizabethville where he had conferred with the secessionist leaders. A day earlier, on October 16, the blockade of the residence was lifted temporarily without explanation. "The Colonel has been brainwashed by the UN," the Commissioner General of Intelligence said. It was at this time, however, that President of the Chamber Joseph Kasongo began to worry. He expressed his fear about the fate reserved for the imprisoned Lumumbist

[10] Jean Finant, Lumumbist leader and President of Orientale Province, was arrested and transferred to Leopoldville. Minister Kashamura and the Muluba leader of Katanga, J. Sendwe, were arrested, then freed on October 19. C. Kamitatu was arrested on November 10 and several Lumumbist leaders, including Finant, Nzuzi, Tshimanga and other associates were in Luzumu Prison in November.

members of parliament in a letter dated October 17 and
addressed to the UN representative in Leopoldville:

Leopoldville, October 17, 1960

Office of the President

Dear Sir:
    I have heard that Colonel Mobutu has stationed a
group of militia from Thysville at Ndjili Airport with
the order to arrest deputies and senators of the Lumumbist group. Given the fact that these persons are accorded
parliamentary immunity, arrests cannot be made without
first obtaining preliminary authorization from the house
they are members of.
    I therefore beg you to station UN soldiers at this place
[Parliament] for the protection of deputies and senators
who are now in the interior of the country and who will
be returning immediately to Leopoldville.
    Would you also kindly ask Colonel Mobutu to tell you
where these innocent victims are being held.
    I thank you in advance for your kind help in this
matter.

With highest regards,
(*signed*)   The President of the Chamber,
J. Kasongo

    The Colonel's attitude was again evident in the begin-
ning of November when rumors about Lumumba's departure to Beirut were circulating: "I will not stop him
from leaving the Congo." The Board itself was still determined to proceed with Lumumba's arrest; in November, they went as far as a de facto breaking of relations
with Ghana, accusing her of "playing the role of principal
intermediary between Lumumba and his foreign con-
tacts." Relations were also broken with the U.A.R.,
which was accused of supporting "rebellious elements."

Finally, Morocco was also accused of having planned to aid Lumumba to leave Leopoldville for foreign lands.

In the middle of November, the chances of a reconciliation seemed to be dwindling. The anti-Lumumbist group at the UN achieved an important victory, thanks to President Kasavubu's action. Back in Leopoldville, the Lumumbist elements—especially the Ghanaians—were in a very difficult diplomatic position, while in Luzumu, several MNC leaders and members were imprisoned.

On the other hand, in Stanleyville, the Lumumbists won some points: with Antoine Gizenga and an ANC group which was pro-Lumumba (the third grouping), they controlled the situation in Orientale Province.

Moise Tshombe.
--Jeune Afrique (Dalmas)

Victor Nendaka of the Congolese Sûreté (left) and Godefroid Munongo, Moise Tshombe's second-in-command. *--Spécial*

Rumors About a Departure

It was at this time that Patrice Lumumba decided that Lumumbist ministers and leaders whose lives were threatened should return to Stanleyville by whatever method possible. According to Kashamura[11] "a small group of trustworthy men" met at Kamitatu's house on November 24. The Provincial President of the PSA promised them assistance in Kwilu and protection against possible prosecutions. "Kamitatu was to stick to the letter of his agreement," Kashamura concluded. The Céréa leader supposedly left Leopoldville after a conversation with Lumumba, who was reported to have said to him, "Anicet, you must precede me. I don't want you to be a martyr."

During this period, rumors about a departure or escape by Lumumba to Orientale Province were circulating. J. Cordy, correspondent of the Brussels *Le Soir,* alluded to this on November 19. Furthermore, *France-Presse* noted on November 25: "Patrice Lumumba will attempt to escape from his residence in Leopoldville and head for Stanleyville."[12]

The rumors fed on reports of the death in Switzerland

[11] In *Jeune Afrique*, no. 168, January 27–February 2, 1964.
[12] In his book, *De Lumumba aux colonels*, A. Kashamura states that an Italian doctor, Dr. Manca, suggested to Lumumba that he go to Switzerland at the same time as his wife, at the beginning of November.

on November 18 of Lumumba's youngest daughter, Christine, whom her father had never seen.[13] On November 20, the Congolese prime minister asked the UN to put a plane at his family's disposal to fly Christine's body to Stanleyville. The petition was denied.[14] Finally the coffin was sent by commercial airliner to Luluabourg, but the police prevented Madame Lumumba from boarding the Air-Congo plane whose destination was the capital of Kasai.

After the departure of Lumumba, an unsigned communiqué written on stationery without a letterhead was given to the press by "Congolese distributors" who guaranteed its authenticity. The Congolese prime minister affirmed in the letter that he was leaving Leopoldville for only "a limited period of time" for strictly family reasons. He would return, he said, for the national Round Table which he would take part in "as Prime Minister of the only legitimate government, along with Moise Tshombe, President of the provincial Katangese government." Patrice Lumumba also declared himself a "dedicated partisan of national reconciliation," pleased with the idea of finding his brothers in battle at the Round Table, and hoping to meet with Joseph Kasavubu shortly. "I have never envisaged my departure from Leopoldville as that of a fugitive," he further specified.

[13] Apropos of the departure to Cairo of Lumumba's three children—François, Patrice, and Juliana—the newspaper *Bingo* of Brazzaville (March, 1964) told of the role played by Abdel Arik Ishak, Counsellor of the U.A.R. Embassy in Leopoldville: the three children journeyed to Cairo by way of Lisbon and Geneva.

[14] Dayal Report to Mr. Hammarskjöld, December 3, 1960.

The Chase

The alert on Patrice Lumumba's departure on the evening of November 27 was quickly given to the staff headquarters of the ANC: "No airplane is to take off from Ndjili" was the instruction given to the UN. On the other hand, it seems that no plan to begin pursuit immediately or to set up roadblocks was put into effect. The officials did not really worry about the escape until Monday afternoon upon their return from Brazzaville, where they were the guests of Abbé Youlou during the independence parade. It seems that President Kasavubu himself did not learn of the flight until Monday at 11 A.M. in Brazzaville.

Having crossed the Kwango by ferryboat, Lumumba's small convoy—a Chevrolet stationwagon, a Peugeot, and a Fiat—continued toward Kenge. At 9 A.M. they ran into the old MNC militant Georges Grenfell, Minister of State, whose car had stalled. The fugitives soon learned that there had been incidents between the Kwango military and ANC men sent from Leopoldville.

Around 11 A.M. the Fiat and Peugeot arrived as scouts at a ferryboat operation run by Kwango soldiers hostile to Leopoldville authorities, whom they suspected wanted to disarm them.

A misunderstanding ensued as soon as the occupants spoke to them of the presence of Patrice Lumumba; the soldiers arrested the passengers, brought them to the Kenge Camp and incarcerated them until 5 P.M. They were all beaten, except for Diaka, who protected himself with the ivory cane and briefcase belonging to his prime minister.

Thanks to the kindness of the Kenge Commissioner, Lumumba finally learned of the misfortune of his companions and was able to liberate them. The atmosphere then changed entirely. Patrice Lumumba and his companions were given an armed escort—two or three soldiers and a police commissioner, M. Lakobowoma—and a truck filled with barrels of gasoline. Thus, around 7 P.M., the convoy left Kenge for Masi Manimba. The territorial administrator welcomed the fugitives there around 9:30 or 10 P.M.; he advised them to continue on their way without delay, but Lumumba's wife and child were hungry. Patrice Lumumba himself did not eat, but the departure was delayed an hour.

The fugitives then traveled to Bulungu, arriving on the morning of Tuesday the twenty-ninth, their truck having broken down along the way.

There the fugitives hoped to buy provisions, but an inhabitant recognized Lumumba. The news spread like wildfire and at 10:30 A.M., Patrice Lumumba was practically forced to hold a public meeting in the center of Bulungu before a very enthusiastic African crowd. He spoke of his difficulties in Leopoldville and explained that he was not going to Stanleyville as a fugitive but to take charge of the liberation of the national territory and the protection of the people.

It was from Bulungu that the first news leakage occurred, permitting the authorities to pinpoint the fugitives. No doubt it was through a radio system, nor-

mally used by private companies, but which also might
have served as a liaison with the ANC. In that case, the
message probably was transmitted to general headquarters in Leopoldville through Tango and Leverville.

The crowd encircled the leader and followed him to the
Pukulu ferryboat, in fact hindering his departure. He
begged the crowd to let him get to Stanleyville without
losing time; once there he promised he would not fail to
help them more effectively. But the village populations
who were informed of his presence forced him to speak
amid great cheering.

From Bulungu, the convoy attempted to reach Mangai.
Traveling on rain-slicked roads, and at night in the
Nkara Sector, they came upon roadblocks set up against
the soldiers and special envoys from Leopoldville. It was
not easy to prove that it was, in fact, Patrice Lumumba
who was with them. The convoy arrived in Mangai on
the thirtieth, in the morning. While there, they had to
repair a car and once again the prime minister spoke to
the crowd. It was not until 4 P.M. that the convoy left
Mangai for Brabanta where, that evening, Lumumba
joined other fugitives: Pierre Mulele, Rémy Mwamba,
Valentin Lubuma,* and Gabriel Yumbu. After a conversation concerning future projects, the fugitives took to the
road again in the night.

On December 1 at 5 A.M., Patrice Lumumba was no
longer in Kwilu. He was in Port-Francqui in Kasai where
the provincial administrator was giving a lunch in his
honor. He himself thought he was almost at the end of
his escapade.

It was nonetheless in Port-Francqui that the first attempted arrest by Congolese soldiers took place. Lumumba wanted to change escorts, but the commander

of the camp, apparently a Muluba, decided to retain the fugitives. Informed of the events, some UN Ghanaian troops intervened, disarming the Congolese soldiers, liberating Patrice Lumumba and taking him with them, assuring him of an escort for about a mile beyond the village in the direction of Mweka.

Some twelve miles from Mweka, the district superintendent, elected officials, and the local authorities welcomed him; the crowd awaiting Lumumba at Mweka wanted to hear him speak. Despite the advice of his companions, Patrice Lumumba agreed to speak. Contact was made at this point with the president of Kasai, Barthélémy Mukenge,* who, by telephone, explained that he was laying the groundwork in Luluabourg. Around 3 o'clock Mukenge sent a telegram, asking that the departure to Luluabourg be delayed, because the army was divided.

On the same day, in Kikwit, Joseph Okito and the Lumumbist deputy Joseph Shako, were arrested, having arrived by chance during the disturbance.[15]

Patrice Lumumba held his meeting at Mweka at 3:30 P.M. Around 4:30 he received a telephone call at the station; he was being called from Luluabourg. At this point he learned of the arrival in Mweka of soldiers from Port-Francqui; he had every reason to suspect them of unfriendly intentions. He left immediately, hoping to confuse his pursuers by taking the fork toward Lodi, at the same time giving the impression that he was going toward Luluabourg.

Along the road to Lodi several flat tires delayed progress, and the majority of the fugitives regrouped in

---

[15] "Okito and Pakassa, part of the Lumumba convoy, were arrested on November 30. Their car was on the way to Tshikapa. They were brought back to Leopoldville." This evidence given in a cable sent to Brussels via Brazzaville on December 2.

Sankuru, near the Lodi ferryboat. These included Lumumba's family, Diaka, Captain Osango, and the small ANC escort from Kenge—M. Kemishanga, Valentin Lubuma, Pierre Mulele, etc. It was then almost 11 P.M. The ferrymen and ferryboat were on the other side of the river. They did not answer the calls. Finally, Patrice Lumumba, Deputy Kemishanga, Lubuma, and Mulele crossed over in a canoe, but they didn't manage to convince the people there of their identities. It was 1 A.M. when the boat finally left. The other fugitives waited on the bank, among them Lumumba's wife Pauline and his son Roland. At this point, the soldiers who had followed them from Mweka caught up with them.

There are several different versions of the events that took place after the arrival of the soldiers. With variations, they fall into the following two descriptions:

1. With full knowledge of the facts and despite his companions' pleadings, Patrice Lumumba managed to convince the ferrymen to cross to the other side of the river in order to try to save his family and friends. He was then immediately arrested.

2. Unaware of the arrival of the soldiers, called from the other bank by those he believed to be friendly, Patrice Lumumba begged the ferrymen to cross back to the other side in the dark and, as soon as he set foot on the bank, he was arrested and brought to Mweka. Apropos of this version, a Congolese witness testified the following to a Soviet interviewer:[16]

About 7 P.M. they reached the village of Lodi where there was a crossing of the Sankuru. There was no ferryboat.

[16] Excerpted from *Patrice Lumumba et la Liberté Africaine*, Editions du Progrès, Moscow, c. 1961.

Lumumba decided to leave the cars and to cross to the other side by canoe. "On the other side we'll find other cars, and if necessary, we'll go by foot," he told his companions. There was only one canoe and Lumumba and three of his companions crossed first in it. His wife and the others stayed on the other side of the river awaiting the ferryboat. When the canoe carrying the Prime Minister arrived at the other side, the pursuers' cars suddenly came into view. The soldiers took the group that had remained behind captive, and called to Lumumba to come back.

Without suspecting anything, Lumumba got the boatmen to return to the other side. When the boat emerged from the darkness, the soldiers jumped aboard, crossed the river, and surrounded Lumumba.

"Chief," said the commander of the group, "we don't want to hurt you. But if we come back without you, we will be killed. Please understand."

Lumumba looked sadly at the soldiers and said, "What's the use of talking. I know that to save yourselves you would kill Pauline and Roland. Kill me then. But remember that you will not be pardoned. And you will regret what you have done today. . . ."

Anicet Kashamura, who was not present when these events took place, published the following account:[17]

At the moment that Lumumba and his family and companions were preparing to board the boat, the soldiers sent by Mobutu arrived on the spot and, without explanation, arrested Lumumba's party, including Lumumba's son Roland. The officials in charge of the boat recommended that Lumumba hide. "No, I can't abandon my son to these men," Lumumba told them. He approached his enemies. There again, facing machine guns, he gave a grand speech, attacking neo-colonialism, imperialism, the missions. He presented his views on the role of the army

[17] *Jeune Afrique*, No. 168, January 27–February 2, 1964.

in an independent Congo. The soldiers declared themselves Lumumbists and decided to leave with him for
Stanleyville. But one of their number caused a sudden
change of heart on the part of his companions. This is how
the Congolese arrested Lumumba.

According to a direct witness, especially well-located
to observe the events and report them objectively, things
happened in the following manner:

The soldiers arrived at the ferry on the Sankuru in an
Opel; there were very few of them (four or five) and
Patrice Lumumba's companions—especially Pauline and
Roland—attempted to find refuge in the forest; the child
began to cry and because the occupants of the car seemed
peaceable, the fugitives came out of the forest, but the
soldiers failed to notice them. They told the people in the
boats, who had finally arrived, that they had come to offer Patrice Lumumba an escort; two or three of them
went across without the car; when the boat reached the
other side, the Congolese prime minister ordered the
others—among them Pierre Mulele—to hide in the forest
and he went to meet the soldiers alone.

On Friday December 2, at 3 A.M., a dispute broke out
between Lumumba and the soldiers: "You don't have the
right to order me around," said the Prime Minister. "It's
not right for you to arrest me. It is I who gave you control in the army, whereas in the Force Publique all control was in the hands of the Europeans. If this earth
drinks my blood, it will mean your own destruction."

The soldiers began to falter in their resolution; but
their commander ended the conversation, and, reinforced by the arrival of a truck loaded with men, the
ANC took the soldiers to Mweka. Patrice Lumumba refused to let any soldier into his car, except those in his
own escort from Kenge, who had, in the meantime, been
disarmed by the soldiers from Port-Francqui.

The convoy with the prisoners arrived in Mweka between 5 and 6 A.M. There, taking advantage of the di-

minished vigilance of the ANC guards, Patrice Lumumba's chauffeur, acting according to orders, raced
toward the UN Ghanaian camp. According to the chauffeur's testimony, the Ghanaian guard, not realizing who
was in the car, barred its passage and a Ghanaian lieutenant who was leaving the camp at that moment told
Patrice Lumumba that it was not his duty to protect him.

Congolese soldiers arrived on the spot at that moment,
and, finding Lumumba leaning against the back of the
car, they beat him with the butts of their rifles and carried
him off. Rebelling against their officers' attitude, Ghanaian soldiers liberated the other fugitives, who were imprisoned in the center of Mweka and were in great danger, but their delayed intervention could no longer save
the Congolese prime minister.

With the Pursuers

During the time that the fugitives were attempting to get to Stanleyville by crossing the Kwilu, what was happening in Leopoldville and in pro-Board of Commissioners circles?

Justin Bomboko and Albert Ndele were absent when the first meeting of the Board of Commissioners took place on November 28. The commissioners received confirmation of the news: "The big rabbit has escaped." At 7 P.M. the Colonel announced that Patrice Lumumba had not yet reached Kikwit, but that "all arrangements have been made for his arrest." Meanwhile, the Board discussed the measures to be taken against Stanleyville, based on the report of Commissioner General of Defense Kazadi, a Muluba of Kasai, who was imprisoned by the provincial Lumumbist authorities in August, 1960, and was liberated only because of Colonel Mobutu's coup d'état.

The next order of business was to name the man who would direct the pursuit of Lumumba and his friends.

He would be Gilbert Pongo. The minutes of the October 17 meeting of the Board defined his position as Inspector of the Sûreté holding the rank of major, and liaison officer. He was also the man behind the arrests of Nzuzi,* Sendwe,* and Mpolo.

"He is the dynamic man we need," Kazadi said of him

on December 5. "And furthermore, he is the only one who has had training in counterespionage in Europe." It was also Pongo who proposed the use of "Katangese officers" to command the troops fighting against Stanleyville, and advocated the elimination of Lumumbism and the severing of relations with all pro-Lumumba countries. On November 28 he reminded his colleagues of "the situation that awaited them if Lumumba came to power."

To be exact, Gilbert Pongo was considered to be an easily excitable agent, having direct dealings with European and American agents. Even before independence, he resoundingly denounced, in the most virulent anti-Communist terms, Congolese nationalist elements, as well as European opinion favorable to an evolution toward independence. For example, he condemned Professor Van Bilsen, author of the "Plan de trente ans" (Thirty-year Plan). In July and August, 1960, he was in contact with circles closest to the Katangese secession and the most violently anti-Lumumbist elements. In mid-September, 1960, in Brussels, Gilbert Pongo made the following threat against a Belgian friend of Patrice Lumumba, Jean Van Lierde: "Tell him that we are going to liquidate Lumumba and that the whites who have supported him will be thrown into the same ditch as he." Belgian witnesses have corroborated this scene.

With Lumumba's escape the group faced the problem of trying to locate him. How could such an operation take place, unless by helicopter, or a special reconnaissance airplane, or perhaps by some as yet unavailable means of transportation?

A first request was made to the UN on Tuesday, November 29 at 4:20 P.M. It originated in Kikwit; Gilbert Pongo, Sûreté agent, had just gone there. The request was denied. Western agents then made offers of assistance to the Congolese Sûreté agents and the Security Services of Katanga and South Kasai were alerted.

A request in due and proper form was then made by Colonel Mobutu to a European airline company. He was supplied with both the machine and the European pilot, a specialist in low altitude reconnaissance flights. The "suspicious" regions were thus patrolled. The first reconnaissance brought the arrest, between Bulungu and Kikwit, of four cars in which the Lumumbists were attempting to escape to Stanleyville.

Lumumba's convoy—three cars and a truck—traveling fast on side roads, were also spotted near Mweka, in Bulongo.

After his arrest, Lumumba spent, according to a European observer, "a very bad fifteen minutes" in the hands of the military. Even though the Leopoldville authorities were informed at this time of his arrest, the only people immediately responsible for his detention at this moment were the ANC soldiers of Port-Francqui. These men were quite incensed and in fact molested the prisoners and threatened to kill them if Leopoldville did not take them into custody before 2 P.M. Orders were given, according to Colonel Mobutu, not to kill Lumumba under any circumstances, and Gilbert Pongo was told to make haste.

Pongo had gone to Tshikapa, believing he might find a trace of the fugitives there; he was in fact told that the prisoners had been spotted on the thirtieth in Idiofa, where they supposedly had stopped for gasoline. Pongo was then detained by the ANC, who took him and his escort for "Kalonjists," a confusion which threatened to become serious at a moment when the tension between

Baluba and Lulua was increasing, following Kalonji's claims that he would extend his state to Tshikapa and Port-Francqui.

Everything proved more difficult than originally expected. Pongo arrived in Luluabourg on Friday, December 2 at 11:10 A.M. by an Air-Congo DC-3; a telegram from the ANC commander of the city addressed to Mobutu had confirmed that the Ghanaian soldiers were bringing Lumumba to Luluabourg, after having delivered him to Port-Francqui. At first Pongo was confined to his hotel, apparently by order of the Provincial President of Kasai, Mukenge, who, we have noted, was in contact with Patrice Lumumba and his companions. The situation was all the more confusing because the ANC was awaiting the arrival in Luluabourg of the UN Ghanaian troops who were protecting Lumumba.

The crew of the plane was thus confined to the Oasis Hotel by the Ghanaian guard of the UN while awaiting directives from Leopoldville. Finally Pongo, after discussions and threats, was able to leave for Port-Francqui, thanks to the aid of elements in the ANC loyal to Colonel Ndjoku,* a friend of Mobutu. In Port-Francqui, Lumumba was handed over to Pongo.

A European who was present at that time, and who had particularly contributed to the apprehension of Lumumba, strongly suggested to Pongo that he immediately transfer Lumumba to Katanga, where he would be judged as a common criminal.

However, the Congolese Sûreté agent stuck to the orders received from his chief, Victor Nendaka, instructing him to bring the prisoner back to Leopoldville.

The Imprisonment

Gilbert Pongo announced his arrival in Ndjili with "the packages" by sending telegrams to Colonel Mobutu and Sûreté chief Victor Nendaka. The Board of Commissioners was also informed, as the official records indicate:

A great many members proposed that Gilbert Pongo be promoted to a higher rank in the army because of his outstanding ability. The meeting ended at 5 P.M. so that certain Commissioners General could go to the air field to view the arrival of "the big rabbit."

The Air-Congo DC-3 landed in Ndjili a little after 5 P.M. and taxied discreetly to the end of the airport, far from the buildings controlled by the UN. Nearly two hundred people were waiting and the vehicle was immediately surrounded by Congolese soldiers, guns leveled at the plane.

Gilbert Pongo—"who made a poor attempt at hiding his triumphant air," as the press agency noted—came down the steps with Lumumba. The latter appeared, hands tied behind his back by a thick rope, wearing a white shirt with the sleeves rolled up—very dignified and showing no reaction, but apparently tired.

The Congolese prime minister and his companions were pushed roughly onto the platform of an ANC truck

where they remained crouching in the very back. In order
to permit the photographers to get some pictures, a soldier brutally raised Lumumba's head, pulling him by the
hair and twisting his arms. According to UN observers,
Lumumba had lost his glasses by this time; his shirt was
stained and he had a clot of blood on his cheek.

Gilbert Pongo personally guarded Lumumba while,
guns aimed at him, some forty soldiers piled into the
truck which took off quickly, followed with some difficulty
by a car loaded with filmmakers and press photographers
and, at the rear, other military vehicles.

The small convoy arrived at the paracommando camp
in Binza where Colonel Mobutu lived, and crossed
through the barbed wire fence, barely slowing down.

While the soldiers were placing Lumumba in a cell in
one of the buildings, they again "roughed him up," according to a journalist who was present, again forcing
him to pose for the photographers, "face contorted with
pain, eyes downcast." The Associated Press gave the following account:

Colonel Mobutu, with folded arms, calmly watched the
soldiers slap and abuse the prisoner, pulling him by his
hair . . . but he was not present when, several moments
later, his soldiers led Lumumba to the improvised prison
in the Binza parachutist camp.

Again according to the same source, quoting eyewitness accounts, Lumumba, arms tied behind him, was
seized by some forty soldiers, thrown to the ground and
hammered by fists and feet, while "Pongo yelled to the
soldiers to hit harder." In the company of several news-
reel cameramen, three other prisoners received the same
treatment. One of the soldiers read aloud Lumumba's re-

cent declaration in which he affirmed his position as legitimate head of the Congolese state. Then the soldier rolled the paper into a ball and stuffed it down Lumumba's throat. The latter did not protest, but grimaced with pain when a soldier "pulled violently on the cord which held his hands tied behind his back." The prisoners were then pushed into an adjoining room where once more they were "savagely beaten." The journalists were not able to see what happened, but they heard screams.

Lumumba in custody.

PART 2
In a Cell at Thysville

Okito and Lumumba.
  ——Dossiers du C.R.I.S.P.

Toward Camp Hardy

According to Colonel Mobutu, the transfer of Patrice Lumumba to the ANC Camp Hardy at Thysville[1] took place on Friday, December 2 at 11 P.M. by a military column including armored trucks. Wounded from recent blows, Lumumba had great difficulty in climbing into the truck.

Thysville is situated in the Bas-Congo about 110 miles from Leopoldville station and was, before independence, one of the most important camps of the Force Publique. It is linked to the capital by an excellent road, which, in times of trouble, can be used by armored and motorized military units. At the time of these events, Camp Hardy was under the leadership of the Congolese superior officer, Colonel Bobozo,* Commander of the Fourth Armored Brigade of the ANC.

One might legitimately ask whether it was during the night of December 2 or 3 that the transfer took place. According to a cable addressed to Brussels and sent in December by the Belgian Embassy in Brazzaville, manifestations of hostility against Lumumba by the soldiers and their wives took place on Saturday December 3 at

[1] Camp Hardy is now called Camp Lieutenant Colonel Ebeya for the high-ranking Congolese officer, chief of staff, killed on February 5, 1964, by the Mulelists of Kwilu.

Nkokolo Camp in Leopoldville, where Lumumba had been taken. The text of the cable was:

[Patrice Lumumba was] very badly treated during the night of the second to the third by commandos who, among other things, burned his beard. Bomboko intervened to restore calm, but without success. According to a sympathetic eyewitness account, the said party [Patrice Lumumba] was actually in very bad condition. He was transferred to Camp Hardy in Thysville, on the afternoon of December 3, by a military column. Guard at Camp Hardy is made up of commandos; we foresee new brutality.

At Camp Hardy, where Patrice Lumumba was incarcerated, there were nine other Lumumbist prisoners. Notable among them were Maurice Mpolo, who was arrested in Mushie while attempting to reach Stanleyville via his native land (Lac Léopold II) ; Joseph Okito, President of the Senate, arrested in Kikwit; and also, for a time, Deputy Grenfell of Stanleyville, who had been Minister of State in the first Congolese government.

Apparently Camp Hardy was not to be the final place of detention until the announced trial. This site, noted *France-Presse* in Leopoldville, would be chosen by the Congolese Sûreté; "His incarceration at Hardy military camp is thus only temporary."

The Detention

Having decided to consider the affair as an interior Congolese problem and not to intervene to prevent the transfer of the prisoner Lumumba from Port-Francqui to Leopoldville and then to Thysville, the Secretary General of the UN nonetheless reacted immediately against the bad treatment that the Prime Minister had received when arrested by the soldiers and then again in Ndjili and Leopoldville. He furthermore protested about the conditions of Lumumba's imprisonment in Thysville.

From Leopoldville, Rajeshwar Dayal, the special representative of Dag Hammarskjöld, wrote:

The UN troops in Thysville have indicated that Patrice Lumumba is being detained at Camp Hardy. They say he is suffering from serious wounds received before his arrival. His head and beard were shaved and his hands remain bound. It is said that the conditions of the cell where he is kept are inhuman as regards health and hygiene.

Mr. Dayal made his impressions known, hoping to convince the International Red Cross to send a representative to Lumumba to see that he be treated "with justice, dignity and humanity."

Hammarskjöld himself considered the arrest illegal; as a member of Parliament Patrice Lumumba was immune to arrest except in the case of a flagrant offense. Yet Congolese authorities not only incarcerated him but also condoned the soldiers' "degrading treatment" of him without ever clearly formulating the juridical basis for his arrest and without ever granting the accused recourse to a lawyer for his defense.

The UN Secretary General did his utmost to see that these appeals were brought to the attention of President Kasavubu, who had left Leopoldville for his native region, the Mayumbe in the Bas-Congo. The initial message would finally be placed in Kasavubu's hands by a UN emissary, who arrived by helicopter in Yshala on December 4.

At the beginning of his imprisonment in Thysville, Lumumba strongly protested the treatment he received. "Lumumba refused all food for a while and people heard him shout, asking for clothes, lodging, and medicine," according to an authorized Belgian observer speaking on December 4 to Belgian authorities. This information radically contradicts Colonel Mobutu's own words to the press on December 6:

Lumumba at Thysville has three boys at his disposal. He sleeps in a very comfortable bed. The ANC spends 1000 francs a day for him and his companions. Two doctors came to see him. The camp soldiers did not want to let them in because they were incensed that so much was being done for Lumumba. . . . Does Mr. Hammarskjöld think Lumumba would have done as much for me if I had been his prisoner?

Colonel Mobutu then declared that he would not authorize the UN to visit the prisoner "as long as the Songolo Question remained unresolved," nor the press, which, he said, "had written hateful and false things."

The two doctors who were supposed to have examined Lumumba and his co-prisoners on December 3 (confirmed on December 7 in a letter sent by Kasavubu to Hammarskjöld) were Belgian doctors: Stephane d'Arenberg, who was Mobutu's personal physician and who was in charge of an International Red Cross mission, and Jean-Pierre de Coninck. Although no communiqué was published by these doctors, the press and President Kasavubu announced that the medical report mentioned a "satisfactory condition." They even added, according to *La Libre Belgique*, that "all the attention required by Lumumba's condition is assured him by a state doctor and nurses." These doctors, using professional secrecy as their reason, have never made public statements or commentaries confirming or denying these allegations.

On December 10, official Leopoldville circles let it be known that Lumumba was not in solitary confinement. "Although closely guarded, the prisoner, as well as his companions, is very well treated. Food is brought in every day from the kitchens of the Cosmopolite Hotel in Thysville."

Very little news about Lumumba's detention in Thysville filtered out. Nonetheless, the wildest and most contradictory rumors circulated during December. For example, it was said that on December 6, the prisoner let Kasavubu know that he would agree to participate in the Round Table and "re-enter the ranks." On the ninth, Gabriel Lassiry,* arriving from Douala, was said to have given Abbé Youlou a letter from Lumumba supporting a reconciliation with Leopoldville authorities; at Christmas, Lumumba was supposed to have been invited to spend Christmas eve with the camp officers; disciplinary meas-

ures were supposedly taken by Colonel Bobozo against
the sentinels who relaxed their surveillance.

On the other hand, a letter, sent to Mr. Dayal, dated
January 4, 1961, and attributed to Patrice Lumumba,
was published by the Yugoslav press organ *Borba* and
was placed in the hands of the UN Peace-Making Commission on January 17, 1961, by Cléophas Kamitatu. The
prisoner wrote:

We live in absolutely impossible and illegal conditions.
The food we receive is bad and insufficient and it often
happens that I eat only one banana in three to four days.
I asked permission to buy fruit with my personal money,
but the military guard refused. I beg you to let my position be known to the Secretary General of the UN whom
I thank for his intervention in my favor.

In any case, contact was maintained with the exterior;
indirect information came notably from the UN Moroc-
cans stationed in Thysville; an Italian firm even put out
a record which contained a declaration from Patrice
Lumumba in Camp Hardy.[2]

A medical delegate from the International Red Cross
supposedly visited Patrice Lumumba and his co-prisoners
in Thysville on December 27. The Red Cross was not able
to procure for us a report of this visit, answering our
request by stating only that "the IRC has the right to re-
serve reports of visits made by delegates to people detained for political reasons for the sole information of the
detaining authorities." It seems, in fact, that the delegate
who visited Lumumba was the Belgian doctor Stephane
d'Arenberg.

---

[2] This text is reproduced in the original French in *La Pensée
Politique de Patrice Lumumba*, Jean Van Lierde, Editions Présence
Africaine, Paris, 1963. Also, see page 167 of this volume.

About the Fate of a Man

In his response of December 7, 1960, to the UN Secretary General, Mr. Kasavubu described his intentions and opinions about Lumumba's fate in the following manner: "It will be our principal concern tomorrow" to assure that the "judicial powers" are able "to hold the trial according to the rules in use in all civilized countries." If this was not immediately possible, it was because the Congo had had its entire court system dismantled, said Kasavubu; and this in large part was due to action taken by Lumumba himself and also because of the special tribunals he organized.

In the meantime, "this man is our legal prisoner, duly imprisoned by a warrant for arrest dated the month of September, 1960, and whose normally rapid execution was only prevented by the UN."

Thus, according to Kasavubu, Patrice Lumumba should be considered to be awaiting judicial action. This action would presumably be based on the following accusations:

1. Usurpation of public functions (Article 123 of the Penal Code)
2. Violation of individual liberty by corporal torture (Article 67 of the Penal Code)
3. Attacks on state security (Article 186 of the Penal Code)

4. Organization of hostile groups with the goal of causing devastation, massacre, or pillage (Articles 193 to
   197 of the Penal Code)
5. Inciting the military to commit infractions (Article
   202 of the Penal Code)

This was also Colonel Mobutu's thesis; he nonetheless
stated on December 2 that "Lumumba will benefit from
normal judicial safeguards when Songolo and the others
have been freed." Alphonse Songolo,* ex-Minister of Communications, had broken with Patrice Lumumba, and had
gone to Orientale Province to take political control there
(according to the prime minister, with the help of American financial aid), but had been imprisoned there and very
badly treated by the Lumumbists. This thesis concerning
the trial awaiting Lumumba was, in principle and publicly, adhered to by all the anti-Lumumbist groups.

"Lumumba should be prosecuted before a High Court
of Justice and answer for the crimes he has perpe-
trated," declared Moise Tshombe on September 6, the
day after the rupture between Kasavubu and Lumumba.
"Lumumba should be judged and should spend several
years in prison for having plunged the country into
chaos," declared Albert Kalonji, President of South
Kasai, on December 25. "Mr. Lumumba will be judged
as quickly as possible. And he will be guaranteed all his
rights," Jean Bolikango, leader of the PUNA party, declared on September 13.

In fact, the matter was neither that clear nor that
simple. Politics in the Congo in December 1960–January
1961 were dominated by interior and exterior factors,
acting in contradictory directions and both greatly affected by the role played by Patrice Lumumba. Thus the
effect of the Round Table on the country's political struc-

ture and on the outcome of the Lumumbist experience in
Stanleyville would depend on whether Lumumba had
played a major political role in one or both. It is easy to
imagine the repercussions that this Round Table could
have on events in Stanleyville; on the future of secession
in Katanga and South Kasai; on the Board of Commissioners General and the personal position of Kasavubu;
on Congolese relations with the most active African
countries and with Western powers; on the political
game of Abbé Youlou and his entourage in Brazzaville;
on the re-establishment of relations with Brussels; on
the behavior of Europeans who stayed on in the Congo
as private citizens or technical assistants, etc. It seems
unlikely that the parties concerned seriously thought that
the problem posed by Lumumba would be easily solved
through normal channels.

At the time of Lumumba's arrest, pressure was already being exerted in favor of sending the prisoner to
Katanga, in spite of secession, and against putting him in
a prison controlled by ANC–Mobutu forces. Even at Port-
Francqui, Gilbert Pongo was strongly advised to act in
this way by a European; it has never been established
whether the latter was acting on his own initiative or in
agreement with anti-Lumumbist elements or groups.

This idea was not abandoned at the time of Lumumba's
return to Leopoldville in early December. Thysville, it
was said, would only be a provisional place of detention
and Victor Nendaka would himself decide upon the final
choice. Brussels was informed on December 3 by an authorized observer that "Leopoldville authorities" would
doubtless try to obtain the accord of the Katangese government, "with a view toward transferring Lumumba to
prison in Katanga." This information, to our knowledge,

did not surprise the Belgian agents involved in the events
in Leopoldville, nor did it cause them to be put on the
alert.

It is hard to be precise concerning which Congolese
authorities are implicated by the cable that we have
quoted, but it would seem at this point that President
Kasavubu was not implicated in the plans for transferring the prisoner. The chief of state had just met Mr.
Tshombe in Brazzaville on November 28 and he had returned to Leopoldville determined not to participate in
the Conference of French-speaking African chiefs of
state, set for December 15 if Mr. Tshombe were going
to be present. Furthermore, the most militant anti-Lumumbist agents thought it necessary to influence Kasavubu through the intermediary of "the progressive Abako
wing," as the Sûreté called it. Mention was made of this
approach in declarations and press articles where the
question of a "safe" imprisonment of Patrice Lumumba
was presented as a test for understanding between Leopoldville and Elizabethville.

"The Leopoldville government is not even capable of
keeping Lumumba prisoner," Evariste Kimba,* at that
time Minister of Foreign Affairs of Katanga, stated de-
fiantly. The day after the interview between Kasavubu and
Tshombe, the special envoy of *La Libre Belgique* wrote
that the arrest of Patrice Lumumba would constitute
"one of the guarantees that [Mr. Tshombe] was doubtlessly awaiting."

During the month of December, no new information
was furnished regarding the transferral of Lumumba,
except in the form of a demand by Kalonji, who had seen
Tshombe again in Brazzaville and who said on Decem-

ber 6: "I asked Colonel Mobutu and President Kasavubu to transfer Lumumba to the central prison of Bakwanga." He was in fact displeased that Lumumba was being kept in an ANC camp when "he is really a common criminal." This is the same Kalonji, who, on October 10, 1960, spoke of the "bloodthirsty Lumumba," accusing him of being "an assassin who must be tried and executed." Later, at the end of December, he declared publicly that in his opinion "Lumumba should not be killed."

The "consul" of South Kasai in Elizabethville, Raphael Bintou,* ex-leader of the FGTK Union and deputy of the MNC–Kalonji in Katanga, said on December 12 that "the traitor Lumumba should be imprisoned forever" and that he would find "a good resting place" in Bakwanga prison.

Moise Tshombe, in a statement dated January 31, 1964, in the weekly *Pourquoi pas?*, affirmed that on November 28 and during December Leopoldville authorities made the first requests for transfers of the prisoners to Katanga.

The idea of transferring the Lumumbists to Katanga, or, in other words, of freeing the political prisoners to their worst enemies, was not an entirely new one.

On October 17, 1960, a Congolese leader speaking to journalists about Félix Moumié, head of the Union des Populations du Cameroun (Union of the Population of the Cameroons) who was known to be in the Congo and was later assassinated in Geneva under very mysterious circumstances, said: "I will do my best to arrest him and send him to the Cameroon government as a present."

As for the transfer of prisoners from Leopoldville to the secessionist state of Katanga, a decision of this sort had been made on September 23, 1960, and the following

telegram had been sent to Tshombe via Brazzaville and
Brussels:

Be advised special Sabena plane will leave Leopoldville
tomorrow Saturday 4 A.M. to transfer several prisoners
Elizabethville prison notably Gizenga and Mpolo STOP
Respectfully

The telegram was signed "Albert Kalonji, Minister of
Justice of the Central Government."

This decision seemed all the more strange to the Belgians because it was attributed to the chief of state and
because it was a question of assuring that not only the imprisonment but also the trial would take place in Katanga.
The only interpretation that the Belgian agent who transmitted this telex message was able to give, by dint of a
real effort of imagination, was that the president "wanted
to give the Katangese moral satisfaction while implicitly
admitting that there was only one legitimate jurisdiction
for all the Congo."

The transfer did not take place and Elizabethville was
advised of the change of program by the same method.
In fact, Mpolo and Gizenga had just been freed. Nonetheless, the fact that this decision was made seems in-
contestable. Commissioner General of the Interior José
Nussbaumer confirmed it in the course of a press conference when he reproached the UN Ghanaian soldiers
for having liberated Gizenga and Mpolo, who were accused of having attempted to corrupt the soldiers in
Camp Leopoldville; furthermore, this liberation took
place "at the time that we were going to transfer them to
Jadotville," according to Nussbaumer.

If it is true, as Tshombe stated, that in the course of
meetings in Brazzaville in 1960 and in the presence of

the chief of state the question of transferring Lumumba to Katanga was discussed, this could only have taken place on November 28, during the celebration of independence of Abbé Youlou's republic or around December 15, at the time of the conference of African chiefs of state of the Brazzaville group.

According to Tshombe—whose revelations in *Pourquoi pas?* were uttered at the time of his battle with Prime Minister Cyrille Adoula—the first meeting between Kasavubu, Ileo, Adoula, and Bomboko on the one hand, and Tshombe and Kimba on the other, took place on November 28, 1960, in the Beach Hotel in Brazzaville. Kalonji was also present. Tshombe said that while at that meeting he was asked by Adoula to agree to the transfer of "Patrice to a safer place" in Katanga, to Jadotville to be precise, and to finish with him. This act would presumably constitute the initial act of understanding between Leopoldville and Elizabethville. It seems that the two Katangese ministers made a counterproposal: "Give us Sendwe" (leader of the Baluba revolt against the Tshombe regime). Kalonji was apparently indignant at the Katangese refusal concerning Lumumba. Victor Nendaka then apparently tried to convince Tshombe, with the aid of a European adviser who told the latter that, to a large degree, Sendwe was only an instrument of Patrice Lumumba. In Masibu village, about eight miles from Brazzaville where Abbé Youlou entertained his guests, President Kasavubu himself again spoke to Tshombe of the Lumumbist danger.

This statement of the Katangese president is quite surprising, to say the least. During the night of the twenty-seventh to the twenty-eighth, the Leopoldville leaders were celebrating Kasavubu's success at the UN.

On the twenty-eighth they were in Brazzaville until 4 P.M., because at 5 P.M. the president was again in Leopoldville. Lumumba was doubtless the main topic of discussion in the course of the festivities in Brazzaville, because that day at 11 A.M. the leaders learned of his escape from Leopoldville.

Either the conversation reported by Tshombe took place after 11 A.M., when the leaders learned of the escape (and in this case, certain statements attributed to Tshombe by his partners in the discussion do not make sense, since they imply that Lumumba was still under military guard in Leopoldville), or as Tshombe affirmed, the discussion took place several hours before the announcement of the escape. But in this case, the supposition would be that the meeting took place at the Beach Hotel around 5 or 6 A.M., and this is not the case.

In any event, neither testimony nor facts confirm Tshombe's narration; his statements, it must be noted, are irreconcilable with the fact that the observers and all the participants took the Kasavubu–Tshombe meeting of November 28 to be a total failure.

What is probable is that besides the above meetings in Brazzaville on November 28, and especially on December 15 and the days following, private meetings about Lumumba's fate doubtless took place among Congolese and Katangese authorities, or even among the advisers to the Congo and Katanga—that is, agents, diplomatic and otherwise, of foreign countries interested in the political neutralization or elimination of Lumumba. In fact, at this time in Brazzaville there were meetings between several foreign agents: French agents such as Charles Delarue (part of Abbé Youlou's entourage) and Colonel

Gillet (chief of Kalonji's army),[3] and Belgian agents and technicians, part of Tshombe's entourage, and that of Colonel Mobutu and Victor Nendaka.

Some of these agents had collaborated before independence with the Sûreté or the Force Publique and still maintained friendly relations with each other—the tone of these relationships not necessarily reflecting feelings prevalent at this time among the Congolese whose advisers they were. At that period, then, a real communications network existed between Leopoldville and Elizabethville, especially at the level of the Sûreté.

This hypothesis concerning parallel discussions on the fate of Patrice Lumumba is quite believable because, within the context of the "common front of moderates" —encouraged by Western agents hopeful of working out a reconciliation between Leopoldville and Elizabethville —the principal unifying factors were opposition to Lumumbism and rejection of the UN proposal calling for elimination of foreign agents and mercenaries (Belgians) in the Congo as well as in Katanga.

According to Luis López Álvarez, a friend of Lumumba's, it was not at Brazzaville but at Pointe Noire that the decisive meeting on the transfer of prisoners took place. According to him, Commissioner Kazadi, and Matuba, a Congolese Sûreté agent, played the important roles.

It was inevitable that the question of Lumumba's fate would be posed while considering the important questions

[3] According to a note of the Katangese Sûreté (No. 304/20/834/-B1/354 dated November 25, 1961), J. Gillet was judged "undesirable" by the Congolese government. He apparently came from Chad in 1957 and arrived in Bakwanga in the beginning of August, 1960. At the end of September, Kalonji employed him as military adviser for the autonomous state of South Kasai.

facing the Congo: the preparation of the Round Table for the regulation of the problem of state institutions; the establishment of a provisional central government which would succeed the Board of Commissioners General; the creation of military and political means to neutralize or defeat Lumumbist forces in Stanleyville; the melding into one power axis of the different leaderships of Leopoldville, Bakwanga, and Elizabethville, an axis which would also include Belgian assistance to the Congo. There were several possibilities for his future: might Lumumba be asked to take part in the Round Table discussion? However, the Kalonjists refused to participate if he were there, and the Katangese refused to see him as anything but the accused before his peers. He could become a third vice-president in the Council in an Ileo government of national unity, as *Le Courrier d'Afrique* suggested. But then, under what conditions and with what risks for those who had divested him of authority in September, 1960? If he was refused a place in the center of the government, or at the Round Table, what might be done with him? Could he be left in the hands of the ANC at Thysville? Until Christmas, no serious risk was evident in that quarter, and this seemed, for moderate Congolese in Leopoldville, a possible solution. Or might he be transferred to a "safer" place, possibly South Kasai or Katanga, thus entrusting him to his worst enemies, who would menace his life? All these questions were posed in Leopoldville, in Bakwanga, in Elizabethville and in Brazzaville.

It is highly unlikely, however, that a proposition in due and proper form—as Tshombe affirmed—was made at this time by responsible authorities in Leopoldville. These authorities consisted of a small nucleus of men made up of Colonel Mobutu, Chief of the Sûreté Nendaka, President of the Board Bomboko, and Vice-President Ndele, acting in close liaison with the chief of state. This group, except perhaps for the head of the ANC, was on particularly bad terms with Tshombe and Kalonji. The latter were attempting to integrate themselves into the Union Douanière Equatoriale (Equatorial Customs Union) and into the group of French-speaking African states whose leadership Abbé Youlou was trying to win. Backed by support from Brazzaville, the two secessionist leaders of Bakwanga and Elizabethville refused all recognition of a central power and a central leader before the Congolese Round Table meeting. The meeting between Kasavubu, Tshombe, Kalonji, and Ileo, held on December 18 in Brazzaville, was particularly stormy, and the Congolese Press Agency decided that this was the moment to announce the rupture between Kalonji and Joseph Ileo.

The question of transferral to Katanga was brought up—the suggestion, as we have mentioned, came from a European and was addressed to Gilbert Pongo on December 2 at Port-Francqui—but explicit orders from Leopoldville were to bring the prisoner to Ndjili and imprison him in Thysville.

The issue was to evolve rapidly after the end of December, 1960.

Toward a New Destination

On Christmas day an important event took place in the east. The Stanleyville Gizengist authorities were able to modify the political course of Bukavu. With the aid of local soldiers, some sixty military and civilian police sent from Stanleyville arrested and kidnapped the head of the Miruho government and the least trustworthy ministers of that government. On January 1, 1961, the attack of the ANC–Mobutu soldiers, led by Gilbert Pongo via Usumbura, was a total failure. Kashamura seized power in Bukavu in the name of the Stanleyville government and Gilbert Pongo himself was a prisoner of the Gizengist authorities.

Simultaneously, the ANC–Lundula was making progress in North Katanga; it gained control of Manono, where a Lualaba government, anti-Tshombist and linked to Stanleyville, was installed by Prosper Mwamba Ilunga* on January 9, 1961.[4] Furthermore, there existed, so it is said, a projected Gizengist offensive to gain control of Coquilhatville by advancing from Yahuma to Boende.

Political confusion was growing in Leopoldville; the Board of Commissioners should, in principle, have been a thing of the past, but on January 1, 1961, it had not yet

---

[4] For the facts about this era, see *Congo 1961*, Benoît Verhaegen, Dossiers du C.R.I.S.P., Brussels, 1962.

been transformed into a provisional government, as
Colonel (soon to be General) Mobutu had hoped, and
no other government had come into being. On the other
hand, the different factions were fighting about the make-
up of the future ministries and the Round Table. In these
struggles—in which the "politicos" were opposed to the
continuation-mutation of the Board of Commissioners;
in which Colonel Mobutu blocked Joseph Ileo and his
formula for a broad national union; in which Jean Bolikango believed his hour as reconciliator/unifier had come
—factions and politicians did not hesitate to envisage or
promise liberation to Lumumba, causing, at the same time,
a hardening of views of those who feared the return of
the Congolese prime minister.

On the international level, pressure in favor of the
liberation of Patrice Lumumba was reinforced in the
UN and at the Casablanca Conference—by the heads of
state of Morocco, Ghana, Mali, and the U.A.R.—who
demanded the liberation of the political prisoners and
the disarmament "of illegal Mobutu bands." The arrival
of the Peace-Making Mission of the UN and Mr. Hammarskjöld in Leopoldville gave some pro-Lumumba partisans the excuse for a public demonstration.

Furthermore, the prospect of the Round Table provoked an uncertainty about the intentions of the authorities; Western observers believed that, under all circumstances, active elements of the Board would remain hostile
to Lumumba's liberation, but they dared not conjecture
about the intentions of the chief of state or, especially,
Joseph Ileo. From Stanleyville came tentative offers for
an exchange of prisoners.

"Gilbert Pongo's safety depends on the immediate
liberation of our Prime Minister, Patrice Lumumba,"

wrote Christophe Gbenye in *Uhuru* on January 10, 1961. And Gilbert Pongo sent message upon message proposing that Lumumba, Fataki, and Finant be liberated immediately in exchange for his own liberation and that of the ANC prisoners detained in Stanleyville.

But it was in Leopoldville itself and in Thysville that there developed the factors that proved the most serious and unsettling for the authorities. The deterioration was all the more serious because it was taking place at the heart of the ANC, that is, the armed force that supported Colonel Mobutu and his Board of Commissioners.

The army was demoralized. The operation against Bukavu had been a rather piteous failure, and there were already new menaces in the province of Equateur as well as in North Katanga. The strongest element in the ANC —the commandos—had been dissolved; one company was sent to Bumba, another to Bukavu, and the hostility of the soldiers toward the commandos who stayed behind was particularly strong. The demands for payment and equipment were bitter. Oppositions and rivalries between the political and tribal factions were developing.

The first sign of tension was manifested in the capital, in Camp Colonel Nkokolo, the former Camp Leopold. There was a serious lack of authority and the officer normally in charge of the camp, Commander Massiala, refused to carry out his orders. On January 7, Commissioner General for Defense Ferdinand Kazadi, a Muluba from Kasai, and General Mobutu went to Camp Nkokolo to straighten out the difficulties. On the tenth, in Paris, Justin Bomboko met with the Belgian representative, Ambassador Rothschild, with whom he hoped to arrange Belgian aid in the form of equipment and soldiers' wages for the ANC–Mobutu. This was to parallel limited re-

sumption of relations between the two countries, the
first stage of which would be an exchange of missions.

During the night of the twelfth–thirteenth, a mutiny
broke out at Thysville, "in Camp Sonankulu and not at
Camp Hardy." The official Belgian observer's word was:
"Patrice Lumumba is still imprisoned in Camp Hardy."
The mutiny was, of course, contagious, and at Camp
Hardy Congolese officers were molested and jailed while
their wives were raped by mutinous soldiers.

To what extent was the fate of Lumumba involved in
the mutiny?

It seemed to be more a question of wages and excessive
inequalities of salary and lodgings between the soldiers
on the one hand and the officers and commandos on the
other. But, as we have shown, the garrison was divided
into opposing political factions. Soldiers—partisans of
Kasavubu and Kalonji—demanded that Lumumba be
removed from the camp and imprisoned elsewhere, where
his presence would not risk causing the ANC trouble.
Others wanted him to return as head of the government
in Leopoldville, and the latter group attempted to exploit
the mutineers in favor of Lumumba. This was, in any
case, one of the reasons that explained the arrest the next
day of some fifty soldiers and the transferral of some forty
others of MNC or PSA sympathies to other units.

Kasavubu, Mobutu, Bomboko, and Nendaka judged the
situation grave enough to rush to Thysville on January
13 "to speak to the soldiers." Bomboko gave a stump
speech promising increased wages, anticipating the as
yet hypothetical financial aid from Belgium.

During this time, the prisoners demonstrated, demanding to see the chief of state, and even succeeded in getting
out of the rooms in which they were kept, breaking the

doors and windows of the building; but they were kept at a distance from the authorities who had come from Leopoldville. Only Patrice Lumumba asked for nothing. His cell was opened by a soldier, but the agitation of the soldiers, as well as the presence of hostile elements, made him fear a trap, and he did not leave the prison. "The officers hoped that Lumumba would attempt to escape, giving them a legitimate reason for shooting him. Patrice was acquainted with this kind of trap," wrote Dominique Desanti about this episode in *Jeune Afrique*—while according to *Uhuru*, the Stanleyville Lumumbist daily, "the garrison . . . had had enough of Mobutu's stratagems and wanted to liberate the Prime Minister; in fact, they almost did just that." The biographer of President Kasavubu, C. A. Gilis, wrote that Patrice Lumumba's cell was opened by mutineers, but because of the hostility of certain soldiers "Lumumba did not dare to risk leaving his cell."

On the thirteenth, in the evening, the Congolese leaders returned to Leopoldville, but in the course of the night and during the day of the fourteenth, it was Camp Nkokolo which was "jumping." A truck carrying soldiers from this camp was intercepted at Thysville and brought back to Leopoldville. Did these soldiers come to liberate Lumumba or, as Colonel Mobutu asserted, simply to make contact with the soldiers at Camp Hardy and learn about Bomboko's promised wages? On the fourteenth, Mobutu himself lectured the troops in order to re-establish calm. And on January 15, in the morning, some soldiers accosted Commissioner General Ndele, who was en route to Rome. They wanted to prevent him from leaving on the pretext that it was he who had held up their wages. According to Victor Nendaka, speaking at that time, even if different political clans at the heart of the army were in conflict, "all the soldiers were united in their anarchy and their demands for wages."

It was in this climate of insecurity that the process was accelerated which would eventually result in the transfer of Patrice Lumumba.

The Commissioner of the Thysville district personally made a trip to Leopoldville at the beginning of January to ask for the transfer of Lumumba to another locality because, he said, his presence caused tension in the region.

According to the text of *Pourquoi pas?*, based on declarations by Tshombe, it was at that time (January 9, 1961) that "Adoula himself, accompanied by Delvaux, came to Elizabethville to attempt to extract from Tshombe's entourage an agreement which would finally move the Katangese president to give in."

This is, of course, an *a posteriori* interpretation implicating Adoula, but founded only on Tshombe's affirmation; the latter was, at the beginning of 1964, attempting to cast a slur on Adoula's political credit.

In fact, it was true that Adoula and Delvaux were in Elizabethville on January 8; they were sent there by Joseph Ileo. The meeting was held to prepare the Round Table which was supposed to open in Leopoldville on January 25 under the presidency of Joseph Ileo and which the Katangese authorities hoped to boycott under the pretext that it wasn't taking place in Elizabethville. At the same time, another mission was sent to Bakwanga with the same goal, while Jean Bolikango was in contact with Stanleyville. Was Lumumba discussed in Elizabethville? Yes, said Moise Tshombe to a conversational partner we can trust, during a discussion that he himself had with Delvaux. The latter—who, we must remember, had, along with Bomboko, countersigned the act of dismissal of Lumumba on September 5, 1960—is supposed to have said to Tshombe that, in his opinion, "only the Katangese can put Lumumba in prison and keep him there." At that time, Delvaux had no governmental or official function in Leopoldville, but he nonetheless discussed with Tshombe the military guard which both governments should provide in common against the ANC–Lundula thrust. Unofficially, Delvaux could be considered a man who had the confidence of the chief of state and a political "notable" in Leopoldville. In a declaration made to Ian Berendsen, the UN representative in Elizabethville at the time of these events, Tshombe himself cited only Delvaux when talking of the request of authorities in Leopoldville "to admit Lumumba to Katanga."

The active role in this affair which was attributed by Tshombe to Adoula constitutes in fact an "addition" whose political significance is quite clear. It also seems that on January 8 and 9 it was not yet the intention of the responsible authorities in Leopoldville to transfer Lumumba to a prison in Katanga. In fact, on January 9 the Board of Commissioners General and Colonel Mobutu favored the plan of transferring Lumumba to Shinkakassa Fort near Boma in the Bas-Congo, because, according to the authorized Belgian observer, "the surveillance will be more relaxed there and danger of contamination of the population almost nil."

This was not just a vague project, for Commissioner of the Interior Damien Kandolo had been in Boma since January 10 with a view toward "preparing transfer of Lumumba [to] Shinkakassa as planned." Brussels was informed of this, in these terms, by an authorized observer.

In fact, the realization of this project was blocked by the refusal of the Commissioner of the Boma district, Oscar Ngoma,* who considered the presence of Lumumba virtually a factor of subversion. This formula thus failed just at the time of the sudden outbreak of mutiny in Thysville and the reaction at Camp Nkokolo.

In Leopoldville, in the anti-Lumumbist faction and among the leaders, panic reigned, especially since January 14 when the newspaper *Présence Congolaise* let it be known that the Lumumbists were preparing to attack the city of Leopoldville between January 21 and 25 to liberate their leader. "Transfer Lumumba [to] Elizabethville . . . for his personal safety and [for] public order in Leopoldville province," recommended the daily, whose directors were closely allied to Joseph Ileo and certain commissioners. At this time, numerous Belgians and Africans were already refugees in Brazzaville, especially after the mutiny in Thysville, and the commissioners were given a military guard for their personal protection.

It was at this moment—January 14—that the Board of Commissioners decided to ask the chief of state to transfer Lumumba "to a safer place." These are the exact words of the official record of the session.

On the same day, a Belgian adviser associated with the Congolese Sûreté gave Brussels a copy of a telegram addressed to Elizabethville. A request was made to Brussels to assist and support "the operation that was envisaged," with the Katangese authorities. Here is the entire text of the telegram; only one word—the name of a commissioner—has been eliminated by us:

Board of Commissioners General takes the liberty of insisting it obtain the agreement transferral of Lumumba to Katanga Province. His presence Camp Hardy risks provoking new trouble. In spite of inevitable inconveniences, it would be wise to agree to authorization transfer to a safe region. Commissioner——insists in the name of his colleagues.

Almost at the same moment a report on the state of the ANC came to Brussels; it was drawn up by a high-ranking Belgian officer, an adviser in Leopoldville. ". . . the value of this army is nil . . . the troops do not obey and do nothing . . . the army even constitutes a danger for the country." Now we must remember that the prisoner, Patrice Lumumba, had been turned over to this army.

On January 15, again according to the same Belgian adviser of the Sûreté, an official request of transit via Brazzaville to Bakwanga had been made by the chief of state to Abbé Fulbert Youlou. This request was reported to have been rejected on January 16 by Brazzaville. It must be noted at this point that Abbé Youlou had just ended a contract with the French agent Charles Delarue "for budgetary reasons."

What had happened? On the fourteenth, in the morning, in this climate of panic, the small "soviet" which constituted the real power at the heart of the Board—assisted by a European agent and an officer, M. Lahaye[5] and Colonel Marlière—had sent messages in different directions in the hope of quickly finding a substitute for the cell in Thysville—again to Boma, but Pinzi* refused; to Brazzaville, but without success; then to Elizabethville, whose reactions are outlined below.

[5] This Belgian agent, a member of the ex-Sûreté of the Congo, had been authorized on October 10, 1960, by the Belgian minister d'Aspremont to accept the function of counselor to D. Kandolo, Commissioner of the Interior.

Having picked up these radio broadcasts, J. Gillet— the ex-colonial of French nationality who had become commander of the Kalonji army of South Kasai, known in code as "Big Kangaroo"—intervened, stating, "If you don't know what to do with him, you can always send him to us."

Thus a project of transfer to Bakwanga had been decided upon, a project which, at first sight, seemed less troublesome than Elizabethville to the Europeans involved in the operation, given the inevitable international repercussions and the degree of involvement of the Belgians in Katanga.

PART 3
Destination Death

Ferdinand Kazadi, Commissioner General of Defense.
——Congopresse

"Les Affreux"—the mercenaries hired by the Katangese govern-
ment to fight the ANC and the Baluba rebels.
——Jeune Afrique (Dalmas)

Preparations for Transfer

The decision to transfer Patrice Lumumba to a place where he would no longer constitute a threat to the Leopoldville authorities was made "at the summit," that is, on the recommendation of the leaders of the Board of Commissioners in agreement with the chief of state. Justin Bomboko, president of the Board and Commissioner General for Foreign Affairs, admitted this implicitly in his telegram of January 21, 1961, to the UN Consultation Committee: "Mr. Lumumba and his friends are and remain in the Congo. Their transfer to Thysville–Elizabethville was not carried out with evil intentions."

Likewise, Joseph Kasavubu on January 28, 1961, in a declaration to the *Radiodiffusion-Television Française*, justified the transfer in the following manner: ". . . because the other prisoners were no longer safe."[1] Kazadi, Commissioner of Defense who effected the transfer, affirmed that he received his orders, orally, from President Kasavubu and Victor Nendaka. Even if the official biography of Joseph Kasavubu does not explicitly mention his intervention, the chief of state has apparently not really attempted to contradict the version of the story

[1] The press of the time reported this declaration, but on June 22, 1966, E. Sablier, director of televised news services at *Radiodiffusion-Television Française*, wrote us that he had been able to find no trace of it, "in spite of all our researches."

81

that implies thàt he took or assumed responsibility for the transfer.

The execution of this decision—choice of place and method of transportation—was in the province of the Congolese Sûreté and the Commissioner of Defense, along with their Belgian advisers.

Following the proposal made by Colonel Gillet of South Kasaì, the Europeans in Leopoldville who were involved in the affair rallied all the more readily to the idea of the transfer to Bakwanga, since the Belgians were less committed to the mining state of South Kasai than to Katanga: the repercussions on the international level would thus be less serious for them. Furthermore, the Baluba of Kalonji would be sure to guard the prisoners quite closely. However, at the same time—on the fourteenth and fifteenth—negotiations were proceeding with the authorities in Elizabethville.

Whatever the place chosen—and everything pointed to its finally being Bakwanga—the transfer would take place by plane. Victor Nendaka and Kazadi, still accompanied by their European advisers, called together the directors of Air-Congo; two pilots of the company, both Europeans, were present.

The plan was as follows: two airplanes would be requisitioned to participate in the operation. A DC-3 would go to Bakwanga, capital of South Kasai, to reconnoiter. The plane carying Lumumba must be prevented from landing at an airport where African troops of the UN would be on guard. A DC-4 would pick up Lumumba in the Bas-Congo. The flight plan given to the control tower of Ndjili Airport would mention only Matadi as destination, so as not to arouse suspicion; but in fact, the possibility of a flight toward Moanda on the Atlantic had already been thought of. It even seems likely that Matadi was only mentioned for form's sake, the real intention being to deposit the prisoner and/or prisoners at Moanda where the UN exercised no control over the installations. From there it would easily be possible to bring the prisoners to Bakwanga. Through an authorized observer in Leopoldville, Brussels was informed that, on the morning of the seventeenth, "departure from Thysville for Moanda" would take place, aboard an Air-Brousse plane; Moanda was chosen "due to the lack of a UN guard."

At dawn on January 17, the pilot of the DC-4, a first officer and a radio operator, waited for Nendaka and Kazadi at Ndjili Airport, while the crew (pilot and radio operator) of the DC-3, the satellite in this operation, were also on hand.

At 6:30 A.M., the DC-4 left Ndjili for Moanda, while at 7 o'clock, the DC-3 took off for Bakwanga, where it arrived after three and one-half hours of flight.

At Ndolo, the old Leopoldville airport, a "Rapid Dragon" belonging to Air-Brousse was preparing to take off for Lukala airfield near Thysville. Commander Jonas Mukamba,* a Muluba of Kasai who had known Lumumba since well before independence and who had visited him three times at Thysville since his imprisonment, boarded the plane. Mukamba was supposed to take charge of the prisoners; he was accompanied by a Congolese Sûreté agent, as well as by an escort of three Baluba of the ANC. At this stage, no European was participating directly in the operation. Kazadi affirmed that, as far as he knew, Victor Nendaka himself went to take charge of the prisoners in Thysville.

Albert Kalonji greeting the Belgian Prime Minister Gaston Eyskens in 1960.

Professor René Clemens, adviser to Moise Tshombe and author of the Constitution of Katanga in secession. —Spécial

Departure from Thysville

In Thysville, at Camp Hardy, two questions were posed by the Leopoldville envoy: will the guards let the prisoners be taken away, and will the prisoners let themselves be taken away without forcing their captors to use violent means?

Few facts are known about this departure. It is not known, for example, who issued the warrant that logically should have been in Jonas Mukamba's hands. In fact, it is not even known whether such a warrant existed, or to what degree Colonel Bobozo, then commander of Camp Hardy and thus responsible for guarding the prisoners, was directly involved in their departure. He had heard his chief, Colonel Mobutu (speaking on January 13 at the time of the mutiny that personally affected Colonel Bobozo and his family), say that it was no longer appropriate that the army be forced to guard political prisoners. It is, therefore, possible that the departure of the three most notorious prisoners under escort seemed to him a simple execution of the wishes of the commander in chief of the ANC.

Whatever the answer, if we depend entirely on the time element, we are led to believe that Victor Nendaka's envoys had to bargain a long time with the guards. It was not, in fact, until 9:30 A.M. that the departure of the "Rapid Dragon" from Lukala to Moanda took place.

Patrice Lumumba and his captive companions did not, it seems, offer any resistance, nor did they refuse to follow Mukamba and his companions.

A journalist, who was, however, not a direct witness of the event, confided to the UN Commission of Inquiry that it was due to a stratagem that the kidnappers were able to act without difficulty. According to his statement, as reported by the Commission, "a delegate of the Congolese Sûreté sent by Nendaka, administrator of the Sûreté in Leopoldville, arrived at the Thysville military camp during the day of January 17 and informed Lumumba and his two companions that there had just been a coup d'état in Leopoldville, that President Kasavubu, Colonel Mobutu, and Ministers Bomboko and Ileo were in prison, and that Lumumba was needed in that city to form a new government. Mr. Lumumba, who was convinced that he would triumph over the crisis, did not doubt for a minute and agreed to leave the garrison."[2]

A second witness who spoke before the commission confirmed this version of the events, describing the strategy employed. The fact is that the prisoners did enter the car which took them to the small Lukala airstrip where the "Rapid Dragon" awaited them.

Another question that this episode poses is: why did the envoys from Leopoldville also take Mpolo and Okito?

If the above hypothesis is to be believed, it would then be normal for Lumumba to insist at that time that he be accompanied by faithful companions. Furthermore, both were known as active and influential supporters of Lumumba. Their titles or functions put them very directly in competition with certain influential leaders in Leopold-

[2] Report of the Commission of Inquiry of the UN, Document A/4964 or S/4976 of November 11, 1961.

ville. Mpolo had been promoted to chief of the army by Lumumba in September, 1960, at the time of Colonel Mobutu's coup d'état. Okito had acceded to the presidency of the Senate and with this title was the second most important person in the country since the choice by Kasavubu of Ileo as the man to form a new central government. According to Lumumba, in a letter of November 11, 1960, to the UN, Okito had already been by this date "arbitrarily arrested several times, beaten, and released."

Pius Sapwe, Commissioner of Police in Elizabethville, greeting Moise Tshombe.

Captain Gat of the Belgian Army.
                                    ——Roger Asnong

Godefroid Munongo reviewing the police of Katanga, accompanied by the Belgian Major Protin (at left). ——Roger Asnong

The Wait at Moanda

Since 8 A.M. the DC-4 from Leopoldville had been waiting at Moanda with a reduced crew—a pilot, a first officer, a radio operator, and the two envoys from Leopoldville, Nendaka and Kazadi. The declared destination of the flight had thus been changed; it was said that Matadi was closed because of inclement weather.

The two Congolese leaders went into the airport terminal and a wait of two and a half hours began for them. It was at 10:30 that the "Rapid Dragon" landed after a flight of an hour at a speed of 120 miles per hour. The three prisoners descended, accompanied by two civilians and escorted by three Congolese soldiers. Beginning with the arrival in Moanda, the prisoners were roughed up and their hands tied behind their backs.

At that moment a fact which is essential to the course of events was revealed: the decision taken by the Congolese participants in regard to the point of destination. Mukamba later affirmed—as did Kazadi—that for humanitarian reasons they had specifically advised against the transferral to Bakwanga. Whatever the reason— perhaps for fear of the presence of Ghanaian UN troops at the South Kasai airport—it was decided to transfer the prisoners to Elizabethville, where, there was good reason to believe, they would be accepted. Kazadi, in any case, affirmed that he was officially informed of an

89

agreement made with Tshombe on the transferral to Elizabethville and, for him, the reception and acceptance of the prisoners was certain.

The authorized Belgian observer, communicating later with Brussels by cable, was to say: "We do not know reasons for change of course to Elizabethville." It does, in fact, seem that the European Sûreté advisers believed that the transfer would be to Bakwanga and were surprised by the decision made by Nendaka and Kazadi.

In accordance with the new decision, Victor Nendaka gave orders to the commander of the DC-4; the latter made provisions to have enough fuel for a flight to Elizabethville. The boarding could then take place with the copper capital as destination.

The following people, besides the European crew, boarded the plane: two members of the Board of Commissioners, Ferdinand Kazadi and Jonas Mukamba, both Baluba of Kasai; the three prisoners, Patrice Lumumba, Joseph Okito, and Maurice Mpolo; and the three guards of the escort, soldiers of the ANC, all of them Baluba of Kasai.

Victor Nendaka signaled for departure at 11 A.M. The plane headed south and, turning toward the capital of Katanga, flew over Angola.

No liaison was made between the DC-4 and the DC-3 heading in the direction of Bakwanga. The DC-3 remained in "stand by" position, waiting at the South Kasai airport from noon on. The crew ascertained that, in fact, there was a UN guard composed of Africans there, but it was unable to transmit the information in spite of reiterated appeals. Finally in the afternoon the DC-3 went back to Leopoldville.

The composition of Lumumba's civilian and military

escort was, we have noted, homogeneous from an ethnic point of view. It was entirely composed of Baluba of Kasai. This is doubtlessly explained by the fact that the Baluba were at the time the most passionate enemies of Lumumba; they accused him, in fact, of having launched the bloody military operations against South Kasai in August, 1960, after the secession of this territory was announced by Albert Kalonji and Joseph Ngalula. The choice is further explained by the destination chosen by the European advisers: Bakwanga.

On the day of the departure itself, the authorized Belgian observer communicated with Brussels by cable, stating that Albert Kalonji had given his accord for the transfer to Bakwanga by Commissioner Kazadi, and that, furthermore, the whole operation "is being carried out without the knowledge of the UN and we are taking every usual precaution,"—adding that "we insisted that decent care be taken of Lumumba." This is the same agent who, the next day, was to inform Brussels, again by cable: "DC-4 left Moanda for Bakwanga; we don't know the reasons for the change of destination to Elizabethville."

It must be noted that Kazadi was particularly opposed to the Lumumbists because he had been imprisoned by them under very bad conditions at Luluabourg from August to September, 1960. He was finally liberated by a written order, transmitted by a European messenger, from Colonel Mobutu; he was freed after the military coup d'état and asked to be a member of the Board.

The airplanes used for this mission were, naturally, serviced by European teams which had been commissioned for the job. Among the members of the crew, three names have been cited. One is noted by the UN Commission of Inquiry, which recorded the statement of a pilot named Paul Bauwens. Tshombe, in his statement of January 31, 1964, to *Pourquoi pas?*, also cited the name of Bauwens who was, according to him, the pilot of the DC-4. Speaking of the situation after the arrival of the plane in Elizabethville, the Associated Press cites another name on January 18, 1961; H. Tournaire and R. Bouteaud, in their *Livre Noir du Congo* also list this same man: Commander Pierre van der Meersch, a pilot for Air-Congo, who was a Royal Air Force pilot before the war. The third name was mentioned on February 12 by the *Durban Sunday Times:* Jack Dixon, a South African pilot who was supposedly in Colonel Mobutu's employ. As for Paul Bauwens, he was at that time employed by Sabena in Tripoli, Libya, and was thus not involved in this affair at all.

From Moanda to Elizabethville

In the plane, the prisoners were handcuffed to one row of seats. All three were beaten and ill-treated during the entire trip. Kazadi himself confirmed this in 1966, citing as explanation the brutality of the Congolese military. The prisoners were obliged to kneel one after the other in the central aisle of the cabin while the soldiers beat them with rifle butts and kicked them. One guard, supporting himself against the partition between cabins, gave Lumumba, who was then seated in one of the passenger seats, a kick in the stomach.

The behavior of the escort was such that the airplane crew became upset and nauseated. The sight of the brutality caused the radio operator to vomit; as for the pilot, he attempted to calm the soldiers, whose movements threatened the stability of the plane. The pilot also tried to fathom Kazadi's intentions: was he going to let the prisoners be killed on board? Kazadi replied with indifference that the passengers would be alive when they arrived. Finally, the crew locked themselves in the cockpit.

Lumumba tried to reverse the situation and avoid being delivered into the hands of the Katangese. The escort was composed of men from South Kasai. Lumumba explained that it was not he who had organized the military action and ordered the massacres of the Baluba in August, 1960; *he* was at that moment on an official visit to the U.S. and the staff commander was Colonel Mobutu; *he* would have done everything possible to prevent these massacres if he had been in Leopoldville. The force of his conviction was so strong that Jonas Mukamba later stated before witnesses that he had for a moment thought of not delivering his prisoners to Katangese authorities: "Patrice recognized my voice and begged me to spare him. He called me 'Jonas, my brother' and gave a long monologue recalling our past friendship."

Around four o'clock, the plane approached Elizabethville, after more than five hours of flight, including a one hour loss of time because of a change in time zone between Moanda and Katanga.

Elizabethville, Capital in Secession

At the time the transfer of Lumumba, Mpolo, and Okito was taking place, Katanga had been in secession for six months. The most important personalities in its government were: Tshombe, Munongo,* Kimba, and Kibwe.* The state of Katanga benefited from technical and military assistance from the Belgian government abroad and, locally, from the support of the large mining companies, which, in fact, assured the financing of the government through taxes and exit permit fees. No foreign country recognized this state, but it nonetheless had close relations with Roy Welenski's Federation of Rhodesia and with Abbé Youlou's Congo. It had also managed discreet but effective friendships with South Africa, Portugal, and with Western ex-colonial circles in Africa.[3]

At the beginning of 1961, the dominating worry of the Katangese government was the menace of the Baluba rebels in North Katanga and the Congolese soldiers who had declared their allegiance to the Lumumbists in Stanleyville (the Gizenga government and General Lundula). The mining center of Manono had already fallen and the

[3] For the situation in Katanga, see J. Gérard-Libois' work: *Sécession au Katanga* (*Secession in Katanga*), Dossiers du C.R.I.S.P., Brussels, 1963, and University of Wisconsin Press, 1966.

Balubakat leaders had just installed an anti-Tshombe
government there whose president was Prosper Mwamba
Ilunga.

Confronted with this menace, Katangese authorities
and their private advisers—especially the colonial Georges
Thyssens, who had been cooperating with Tshombe's
Conakat since the creation of this ethno-political group
in 1958—were attempting to reinforce the police by giving it white mercenary units recruited from South Africa
and Europe. At that time, Thyssens was trying to recruit
from France Colonel Trinquier and his friends from the
"Algérie Française" circle. He promised them, in the
name of Moise Tshombe, supreme command of the police,
until then assumed by Belgian officers.

Despite these military weaknesses in the north, the
Katangese authorities had a relatively strong political
position in comparison with that of Leopoldville, where
the Board of Commissioners should, in principle, have
held power but where no government authority had actually emerged. At that time, Leopoldville had just suffered a severe defeat in its attempt to recover a Lumumbist province. In fact, at Bukavu on January 1, 1961, the
ANC–Mobutu troops had been forced to flee while, as we
have seen, a threat of mutiny was developing at Camp
Hardy and in Leopoldville during the first fifteen days
of January.

Under these conditions, Leopoldville became the party
that made demands during its dealings with Katanga
concerning a possible military agreement. This agreement—foreseeing a somewhat fictitious unity of command—would have permitted Tshombe's police to leave
the secessionist province; their excuse would have been
that of combined action against the provinces which

recognized the legitimacy of the Gizenga government in Stanleyville.

The Katangese attitude was rather negative concerning President Kasavubu's project of a Round Table of national reconciliation, whose purpose would be to resolve the Congolese constitutional problem and permit the creation of a provisional central government. Mr. Tshombe refused to participate if the meetings were held in Leopoldville instead of Elizabethville.

At the same time, relations between Katanga and the UN had again deteriorated. The Katangese violently reproached Mr. Berendsen, the UN representative, for having let General Lundula's soldiers pass through a neutral zone whose control devolved upon the *casques bleus*. Furthermore, the authorities in Katanga remembered with bitterness, and as a "sign of complicity" between the UN and the rebels of North Katanga, the authorization previously given to the leader of the Baluba-kat, Jason Sendwe, to go through rebel zones with the supposed purpose of pacification. At the time, the state of Katanga still depended principally on Belgian cadres for the maintenance of order, which was the basis of its political existence. The head of the police was Colonel Crèvecoeur, assisted by Major Perrad. President Tshombe was advised by Major Weber[4] and by a team of Belgians headed by Professor René Clemens of the University of Liège; this team included, notably, R. Grosjean and J. Brassinne, who would again be present in Leopold-ville in 1964. Nearly two hundred and fifty Belgian soldiers—not mercenaries, but under the title of technical

---

[4] Active Belgian officers, like Major Weber, were officially advised by their superiors that the "colonial part" of their career should be a professional secret.

aides—were in the services of the Katangese armed
forces. Some vital institutions, such as the Sûreté, Intelligence, and Communications, functioned quite effectively
due to impressive Belgian assistance. At the Belgian consulate, a strong personality—Colonel van de Waelle, ex-
General Administrator of the Congolese Sûreté under
the Belgian colonial regime—managed to gain control
of several growing administrative functions in a short
time.[5]

In January, 1961, the situation was comparable to
that of November 11, 1960, as described by the Belgian
diplomat Rothschild. "Belgian support," he said, "is an
essential and decisive element for the maintenance of
order in Katanga. Its withdrawal would bring the collapse of the police within twenty-four hours; this would
be followed very closely by the collapse of Tshombe's
government."

Among the Katangese leaders, one man was known to
be especially hostile to Patrice Lumumba: Godefroid
Munongo, Minister of the Interior, first president of the
Conakat. He was such an ardent partisan of the secession
of Katanga that he attempted to secure it even on the
eve of the independence of the Congo at the end of June,
1960. The hostility between Munongo and Lumumba
was evident in several events during 1960. In March,
1960, during the course of a visit by Lumumba to Elizabethville, inflammatory tracts were distributed by his adversaries accusing Lumumba of being an agent of the
Soviets and demanding his immediate expulsion. The
two men had some very harsh words with each other at
this point.

---

[5] It was also he who, in October–November, 1964, created in
Kamina the Fifth Armored Brigade charged with reconquering
Stanleyville.

The failure of the attempt at secession in June, 1960 by Tshombe and Munongo, aided by a Belgian named Sheerlinck, was due to concerted action by Belgian authorities and Prime Minister Lumumba. This failure provoked extreme anger on the part of Munongo against the Congolese "unifiers," especially against Lumumba and Gbenye, his Minister of the Interior, but also against the leaders of the Balubakat.

During the troubles in July, 1960, specifically at 9:30 P.M. on Tuesday the twelfth, Munongo himself forbade a military plane to land at Elizabethville under the pretext that Lumumba was aboard, accompanied by the chief of state. Luano, Elizabethville's airport, was guarded by Belgian troops, and it was then that Katanga began its secession. Munongo's decision, according to the Belgian Major Weber, had "saved order in Katanga."[6]

During the month of August, 1960, Munongo gave instructions to the police that Patrice Lumumba must be prevented at all costs from landing in Katanga, and if he succeeded, in spite of everything, he must *disappear*.

[6] The refusal to allow the plane to land had a deplorable counter-effect in Luluabourg. The agreement given by Lumumba to the Belgian Consulate of that city, authorizing a Belgian military presence which would insure the safety of the Europeans and check their massive departure, was suddenly withdrawn after the Elizabethville episode. (See, *Congo 1960*, Dossiers du C.R.I.S.P., Brussels, 1961.)

"The Three Packages"

Approaching Elizabethville, the pilot of the DC-4 made contact with the Luano control tower: "I have three precious packages on board," he is reported to have said; another version is that he said, "I have three parcels on board."

In accordance with a Tshombe-Hammarskjöld agreement of August 13, 1960, the airport was under the dual control of the *casques bleus* and the Katangese police. But the Luano control tower was managed exclusively by European telecommunications technicians. The commander of the airport, Mr. Dedeken, was at his post. The pilot of the DC-4 asked permission to land as soon as possible, mentioning his short fuel supply, and the plane was then put in a holding pattern.

The chief staff officer of the Katangese police received a telephone message from the control tower: "Three big packages are going to arrive." The Belgian officer, Major P., in charge of staff headquarters, attempted to reach Moise Tshombe by telephone, but the latter was not home; he was in fact at the Ciné Palace, opposite the main post office in Elizabethville, attending a showing of the film *Liberté*, made by Moral Rearmament. In Tshombe's absence, headquarters reached Munongo. An armed escort was immediately ordered to be at the airport and Munongo rushed there.

Here a key question must be posed: Were the authorities in Elizabethville waiting for the prisoners and had they given their permission for the transfer?

The clues, it should be noted, are not clear on this particular subject. Apparently, the Katangese authorities were not awaiting the arrival of the prisoners *at that particular moment*, otherwise Munongo would have been at Luano and it would not have been necessary to make the plane wait before landing. Also, Moise Tshombe would doubtless have been waiting at his home so that he could be contacted.

If the prisoners were not expected at that moment, did the authorities in Elizabethville at least know that the transfer might take place, and did the Katangese authorities agree to it? And if so, which ones?

According to Berendsen, Tshombe said that he had been approached by Albert Delvaux, ex-minister and delegate from Leopoldville, who supposedly begged him "once again . . . to admit Lumumba into Katanga." Using this opportunity, the Katangese government had decided to examine the question. "However," Tshombe added, "no definite agreement existed between the two governments on this subject at the moment when Katangese authorities were informed that an airplane carrying the prisoners was landing in Elizabethville."[7]

The Katangese authorities at least admitted, then, that discussions were being held. On January 19, 1961, a communiqué from the Katangese Intelligence Service to the press and radio stated:

At the request of President Kasavubu, and with the accord of the Katangese government, Patrice Lumumba

[7] Documents of the UN A/4964 and S/4976 of November 11, 1961; Report of the Commission of Inquiry.

the traitor has been transferred to Katanga, Thysville prison no longer offering sufficient guarantees for his safety.

Doubtless such a text could be considered, *a posteriori*, as a proof of the existence of a Katangese agreement made *before* the transfer. But it could also, in fact, be the result of a decision tending to legitimize at that moment the acceptance of the prisoners by the Katangese. Later, in fact, in his statements in *Pourquoi pas?*, Tshombe claimed to have learned of the arrival of the "three packages" through Kasavubu, by telephone, at the moment that the DC-4 was landing and was completely unaware of the meaning of the message. Refusal to admit Lumumba into Katanga was, he stated, "without appeal."

In order to see things clearly, we must review the complete chronology of events. In December, 1960, the goal was to transfer Lumumba to a province or region which would be "safer" (from the Leopoldville authorities' point of view) ; however, nothing indicates that at that time they would have gone as far as formulating a serious project to which the authorities in Elizabethville would have formally committed themselves. We have spoken of these discussions above in Part II. It seems, as was revealed by the official report of the interrogation after his arrest in April, 1961, in Coquilhatville, that Tshombe had, at this time, "always said that he [Lumumba] should go to Bakwanga while [Tshombe] was especially interested in Sendwe's fate." Tshombe's very words, which he himself reported to the people in Leopoldville, were: "Give us Sendwe. We have an account to settle with him."[8] Apropos of Sendwe, Munongo himself told

[8] *Pourquoi pas?*, January 31, 1964.

a visitor from Kasai on January 28, 1961, of his desire to hang him in Elizabethville.

It is probable that Mr. Delvaux brought up the problem of the transfer of Lumumba during his visit to Elizabethville on January 8, 1961. Mr. Tshombe admitted to Mr. Berendsen that he had not responded negatively, but had agreed to examine the proposal closely. What is not stated by Tshombe in his declaration to Mr. Berendsen is that there were other quite pressing demands on the morning of January 14, 1961; this was after Leopoldville had learned of the danger of mutiny in Thysville and understood that any small event might suffice to put Lumumba back in power. Up until January 10, 1961, in fact, Lumumba's presence at Thysville, some twelve miles from the capital, constituted in itself a serious obstacle to the Round Table and to the constitution of a central government of supposedly moderate tendencies. But after the serious events of January 13 in Thysville, the risk of his presence became immediate.

The telegram we published in Part II[9] noting the request made by a competent commissioner indicates that the Elizabethville authorities were barraged with petitions to transfer Lumumba and that Brussels was aware of them.

It is also true that a meeting of the "inner cabinet" was held in Elizabethville and was attended by Tshombe and his principal Belgian advisers—Weber, Clemens,[10] as well as the head of the police, and at least two minis-

[9] See page 76.
[10] The professor was, despite UN orders of expulsion, at Tshombe's side until the end of the Katangese secession, and he still carried out his functions as private adviser when Tshombe became prime minister in Leopoldville in 1964. Mr. Clemens was also among the first persons asked to leave the Congo by the Kimba government in 1965.

ters, Munongo and Kibwe. The cabinet was consulted on what response to give Leopoldville. A majority did not favor a transfer because they felt it would complicate even further the politics of the state of Katanga. Munongo, however, would willingly have assumed the risks of the transfer, but some members of the cabinet left the meeting with the impression that the answer to Leopoldville would be negative.

In fact, the first answer *was* negative, but the same day a second message was sent to Leopoldville; Elizabethville would accept Lumumba if the Balubakat leader, Jason Sendwe, was also in the same plane. This unreasonable demand provoked a lively opposition in Kasavubu's cabinet, notably by G. Denis, the Juridical Counselor, and it was at this time that a decision seems to have been reached about the transfer to Bakwanga. The question of the transfer, or at least the arrest, of Jason Sendwe was later posed by Elizabethville as a side issue during the discussions concerning a military agreement. But Bomboko again rejected this Katangese demand on January 28, 1961.

Our records contain a piece of information which, if its authenticity could be confirmed, would be decisive: a letter from Tshombe to Justin Bomboko, President of the Board of Commissioners, dated January 15, 1961, in which the Katangese leader writes:

Apropos the message that we have just received, we agree to the immediate transfer of Lumumba the Communist to Elizabethville. This operation must be carried out secretly. Would you advise us of his arrival as soon as possible?

This document, published by *Jeune Afrique* in its October 4, 1964, issue, was circulated at this time by the

Ligue de la Resurrection Congolaise (League of Congolese Resurrection), a group operating out of Zanzibar. The accompanying text, written in very primitive French, gave the important European figures who were linked to the secession an excuse for calling it a forgery; but if it is, it is a remarkable imitation, not only because of the signature, which is exactly like Mr. Tshombe's, but also because of the reference number, which dates it as being written on January 15, 1961, and fits it perfectly in the order of numbered letters and notes of the Katangese presidency. The question is still not settled when we further affirm that this letter would contradict the decision taken by the inner cabinet "weighted" in favor of the responsible European element. Furthermore, this is not the only example of a text of this nature.

In any case, a high Katangese functionary, speaking to the UN Commission of Inquiry, asserted that he knew of a positive response by Mr. Tshombe dated January 15 in answer to a request made by Kasavubu or Mobutu on the same day. As concerns the role of Colonel Mobutu in this affair, two contradictory versions have been advanced. Edouard Mendiaux, a moving spirit of Amities Katangaises (Friends of the Katangese) in Belgium and an ardent partisan of Tshombe, wrote in the daily *La Libre Belgique* issue of April 1–2, 1961: "Colonel Mobutu is in contact with the President of Katanga, Tshombe, who agrees to accept the captive [Patrice Lumumba] in Katanga." On the other hand, the biographer of Colonel Mobutu, his friend Francis Monheim, wrote: "No one spoke of a possible transfer of Lumumba to the Katangese capital . . . the thing was decided in top secrecy and they did not keep the Colonel informed of their decision." Monheim concluded that "Colonel

Mobutu seems to have been betrayed by several of his friends."[11]

What is certain is that following the demand from Leopoldville on January 14, Elizabethville answered affirmatively at least once but demanded at the same time the transfer of Sendwe by the same plane, a condition rejected by Leopoldville. It is possible that a later letter from Mr. Tshombe dated January 15 was really addressed to Bomboko, agreeing this time to the transfer of Lumumba unconditionally; but the means of verifying the authenticity of this letter are lacking. It is equally certain that subsequently, that is, on January 17, by deciding to avoid Bakwanga and send the prisoners to Elizabethville, both Nendaka and Kazadi at least had an idea that they would be admitted.

What is also certain is that Brussels received a telex message on January 18, 1961, from their consul in Elizabethville stating "the authorities were surprised by this sudden but expected arrival." It seems that therein lies the true explanation. The transfer was expected, but the moment had not been set and the arrival was *sudden*.

[11] *Mobutu, l'homme seul.* Francis Monheim, ed., Editions Actuelles, Brussels, 1962.

A short time after Lumumba's death, Abbé Youlou arrives in Elizabethville. Tshombe is escorted by the Belgian major Weber.

—UPI (Steiner)

Kasavubu is greeted by Abbé Fulbert Youlou, President of Congo-Brazzaville, in Brazzaville, December 15, 1960.

—Congopresse

At Luano

It was 4:45 P.M. when the airplane, having received the go-ahead from the control tower, landed at Luano.

The exact hour is stated in Appendix Two of the *Bulletin of Information of the State of Katanga,* number 91, of January 18, 1961. Surprisingly, the initials P.L. are modestly inscribed in the column where the number of passengers is normally listed.

Godefroid Munongo had arrived at the airfield and took up his station at the control tower. The office chief, Mr. Tignée, ex-colonial administrator in Baudouinville, was also there.[12]

Since the airport had become by that time a sort of "forum" for Elizabethville, several Europeans were present at Luano when the Air-Congo DC-4 arrived, but some were there merely because of their jobs and others quite by chance. It was not always easy to determine why they were there, especially when it was an important European who, as other sources indicate, had often attended council meetings of the Katangese ministers—or, further, when it was a man from G2 (Intelligence Services), who went to the president's house every day. Several of these Europeans were quite far from the runway itself, behind the fence that surrounded the terrace of the restaurant

---

[12] Mr. Tignée was to be on the first list of advisers expelled by the UN at the beginning of August, 1961.

or in the main building of the airport. A DC-4 arriving from Luluabourg was expected any moment; it would, in fact, land at 5:15 P.M.

The units called by Munongo to insure the success of the operation belonged to the first company of the police; there were a total of about forty men, commanded by European cadres—eight officers and warrant officers. Who were these men? There was Captain Gat, a Belgian officer in the service of Katanga in the division of technical military assistance.[13] His name has often been cited in speaking of this affair. Other names often come up in the accounts which have been given of the event: Michel, Léva, and Rouchefort were mentioned in *Jeune Afrique* on June 13, 1965; Léva and Rouchefort were mentioned in *Révolution Africaine* on January 15, 1966; Lieutenant M. ———, Second Lieutenant L. ———, and Sergeant Major R. ———, were listed with discretion in *Le Dossier du Mois* of October, 1964; Lieutenant Grandelet was noted in *Auto-Journal* of April 6, 1961. Thus the men who were in command and served as cadres in the military police were mostly ex-members of the Force Publique or "European volunteers."

The presence of two ministers, Kitenge and Kibwe, has been cited by the Katangese authorities, but the fact has not been formally established, unless one accepts the testimony of Kazadi, who says that Kibwe was there. Pius Sapwe,* Chief of Police of Elizabethville, was also present.

Arriving from Elizabethville, the civilian and military police went directly to the military installations and

---

[13] Gat was photographed in 1965 by a special envoy of *Jeune Afrique* in front of his house near Anvers; he is still in the Belgian Army.

hangars reserved for the Katangese planes, "Aviakat," thus avoiding the UN-controlled areas. The control tower also directed the plane, after a normal landing, toward the Aviakat airstrip.

After coming to a halt, the DC-4 was surrounded by a cordon of Katangese guards. In the distance, the Swedish *casques bleus* watched this deployment of force impassively—or powerlessly.

Close-up of the death house. This photo, made public by Godefroid Munongo, was supposed to represent the hole made by Lumumba, Okito, and Mpolo when they attempted to escape.
——Associated Press (Wide World Photos)

The Prisoners Are Handed Over to the Katangese

There are many diverse eyewitness accounts concerning the disembarkation of the prisoners and their physical condition at the time they were handed over to the Katangese guards.

According to Berendsen, who did not learn of the events until an hour or two after the arrival of the prisoners but who then personally proceeded to interrogate the UN guards, the Katangese forces included more than one hundred persons. The *casques bleus* were at a distance of 50–100 yards but could not approach because of the cordon set up by the Katangese. The prisoners had their hands tied behind their backs and their eyes were blindfolded; they were beaten upon their arrival and as they landed they were struck with rifle butts by the police. They were then quickly led away in jeeps.

This version is obviously founded on the declarations of the head of the Swedish guard at Luano, Warrant Officer Lindgren:

On January 17, a DC-4 Air-Congo plane, having landed, taxied directly to the Katangese Military Air Force hangar which was not part of the zone patrolled by the UN company stationed at the airport. An armored vehicle, some trucks, and jeeps surrounded the airplane

113

and the Katangese police formed a cordon about eighty
yards away from the airplane. Some twenty policemen
formed a solid line between the airplane and a jeep which
had pulled up, and the armored vehicle pointed its can-
non toward the door of the plane. The first passenger to
leave the plane was a well-dressed African; he was followed by three other Africans, whose eyes were blindfolded and whose hands were tied behind their backs.
The first of them had a small beard. The moment they
descended the steps, the troopers rushed toward them,
hit them, beat them with the butts of rifles, and threw
them into the jeep. Four policemen then jumped into the
jeep and sat down. At that moment one of the prisoners
let out a piercing scream. Then the jeep left at the head
of a military convoy which went to the far border of the
airfield, driving through a hole in the fence, and disappeared into the distance.

As a result of the tension existing at the time of these
events between the Katangese authorities and the UN,
the Swedish guard did not attempt to approach the
hangars of the military air force; the UN post was, in
any case, at the foot of the control tower, that is, about
245 yards from the military airstrip. The incomplete
and imprecise nature of the testimony gathered from this
group can be explained by this fact.

However, according to the testimonies we have gathered, it is possible to put the facts together accurately.

After the DC-4 had come to a halt on the Aviakat airstrip, a stairway was rolled up to the plane while the
guard took their places. This guard was furnished by the
first company of the military police; the latter counted
among its members certain people whose attitude at the
time of the mutinies at Camp Massart in July, 1960,
was such that it attracted the attention of the Katangese
authorities and the white officer groups. The commander
was, as we have said, Commander Gat. Among the Eu-

ropean officers were Lieutenant Grandelet, Lieutenant Michel, Second Lieutenant Léva, and Sergeant Major Rouchefort, all of Belgian nationality. The officers were ex-members of the Force Publique.

A jeep and a half-track approached and stopped about ten yards from the plane. Two empty trucks waited near the hangars. The military police formed a solid line between the exit of the DC-4 and the vehicles. The 30-caliber machinegun mounted on the half-track was pointed toward the door of the plane.

Commissioner Kazadi was the first to alight,[14] followed, according to him, by Mukamba. Not one member of the Air-Congo crew appeared at the door, as is generally the case after landing. (The UN at that time occupied the airport buildings [tower, lobby, offices] while the police controlled the Aviakat hangars. The fire equipment was used for both military and civilian airplanes, UN as well as Katangese.) The three prisoners followed directly behind. Patrice Lumumba had his hands tied behind his back. He was wearing a white shirt without a jacket and had no glasses. He was bleeding and his face was swollen. Members of the ANC who made up the escort pushed the three men toward the stairway. According to witnesses who were less than ten yards away, the prisoners, especially Lumumba, who was in bad shape, were thrown to the ground as soon as they appeared at the door of the DC-4. At that precise moment, a voice was said to have cried: "They must not dirty the Katangese soil." Other witnesses declared that the prisoners descended from the plane unaided.

In his statements in *Pourquoi pas?* of January 31, 1964, Mr. Tshombe tended to credit as correct the version

[14] An eyewitness, however, said that the first to alight was a tall Congolese lieutenant, a member of the escort.

which maintained that the prisoners were already mor-
tally wounded at that point by the blows of the Baluba
escort. According to the Katangese president, it was
Kazadi himself who set the tone by slapping the prisoners
and exhibiting at Luano "with an unconscious and cruel
pride, the mustache, beard, and glasses of Patrice Lumumba." The Belgian journalist Pierre Davister wrote,
on January 20, 1961, that "to all those who could recognize Patrice Lumumba from a distance, it seemed that
he had a curious bandage on his eyes [and that] Mobutu's
soldiers immediately began a lively spectacle by shower-
ing Lumumba with blows from the butts of their rifles
and literally [throwing] the prisoners into a jeep."

Were the prisoners almost dead at that point?

The explanation given by the Katangese authorities is
rather belated and does not correspond to the facts. The
prisoners were doubtlessly weakened by the blows they
received in the airplane, but nothing suggests that these
blows were mortal.[15] Photos of the arrival supposedly
exist; this is possible, but we could find no trace of them.
A Belgian journalist, Gaston Bunnens, has written in
Germinal, and confirmed to us, that he saw a photograph
showing Patrice Lumumba at Tshombe's feet; but he no
longer remembers who showed it to him nor does he pos-
sess a copy. It is possible that a Belgian agent of the
Katangese Intelligence services was present and photographed Lumumba after his arrival in Elizabethville. In
any case, he has not released the photo.

According to a telex message from the Belgian consul
addressed to Brussels at the time of the events, it was

---

[15] This does not however authorize us to accept J. Bomboko's
allegation, expressed in a telegram to the UN Commission of Inquiry on the Congo (1/21/61), that "the rumors that the prisoners
had been molested" must be denied and that the prisoners were
"quite well."

part of the intention of "Minister Munongo and his Chief of Cabinet Tignée [to have Lumumba] examined by a doctor to discover the state in which he had been brought to Katanga." In any case, this message does not allude to a serious condition and uses the adjective "molested" when speaking of the prisoners upon their arrival. For his part, Kazadi firmly maintained that the prisoners, though certainly beaten up in the airplane, were in no way near death upon their arrival.

As soon as the prisoners set foot on the airstrip— all accounts agree on this point—the police struck them and they were pushed some ten to fifteen yards before being thrown into the jeep. Four policemen sat on the prisoners. At that point, according to Lindgren's testimony, one of the three prisoners let out a piercing cry. Patrice Lumumba, said a witness, did not speak, thus demonstrating his courage. He did not cry out at that moment. However, the Belgian consul affirmed on January 18 in Brussels that it was "inaccurate to say that he was struck violently in Elizabethville either by white officers or the Katangese police."

Munongo was present at the operation, calmer than the journalists have generally described him to be. The same Katangese policemen, commanded by the same European officers, then escorted the jeep toward the southwest border of the airstrip; the convoy traveled alongside the runway and continued toward the edge of the airport, where normally there was neither entrance nor exit.

All in all, the operation did not take longer than three or four minutes.

The convoy left the airport by a dirt road, through the airport fence which had been cut into sections to permit the passage of vehicles.

The ANC escort, relieved of its duties, remained on the

Aviakat airstrip. Later, the Katangese police took these Congolese soldiers to Camp Massart; their tribal origin and their membership in the Leopoldville army did not make their welcome there particularly warm. The next day, the Baluba soldiers in the escort were brought back to Luano and they returned to Leopoldville aboard the Air-Congo DC-4. The plane, with the same crew, took off at 9:30 A.M., local time. Commissioners Kazadi and Mukamba dined in town at the house of a Muluba tribesman from Kasai, Cléophas Mukeba, and stayed at J. B. Kibwe's house; the latter, according to Kazadi, did not come home during the night of the seventeenth to the eighteenth. They left Elizabethville the next day. Kazadi left Tshombe on the morning of the eighteenth, and the Katangese president supposedly told him that he had seen the three men and added, "Everything is fine, they are prisoners."

Toward the Place
of Detention

After having gone through the space in the fence, the convoy carrying the prisoners took the right fork of the two roads leading to Elizabethville. The scenery changed; now the landscape consisted of high grass and stunted trees. The convoy passed in front of three clay houses occupied by villagers and then reached a crossroad. On the right now were the stables and buildings of a riding club belonging to a Mr. Verlaine.[16] Then on the left was a place called "Le Pondoir" (Chicken Coop) and property belonging to a Belgian colonist, Mr. Browez; this house has long been thought to be the house of Lumumba's imprisonment and death.

Driving by the crossroad the convoy entered a wide dirt road leading to Elizabethville. There, after proceeding several hundred yards, the convoy stopped in front of a house on the left side of the road. The convoy had traveled 2.3 miles. Some ten minutes had passed since the departure from the Aviakat airstrip.

The house, like "Le Pondoir," belonged to Mr. Browez,

[16] Testifying before the UN Commission of Inquiry, a Katangese witness and close collaborator of Tshombe declared that it was "in a kind of riding club" or rather "a bar which also serves as a kind of riding club" that Patrice Lumumba was imprisoned upon his arrival. The confusion is understandable.

who was abroad at the time. It seems that the Katangese had intended to incarcerate the prisoners with all possible speed; they chose an unoccupied residence, two and a half miles from the city yet close to the airport. It was here that the last act of Patrice Lumumba's life was to be played out, and not, as has been erroneously written, in one of the so-called "Sabena" houses. These houses, situated along the Elizabethville–Luano road and theoretically destined for the Air-Congo personnel, were already occupied at that time by UN personnel.

The Browez property was situated some twenty yards from the road, near a high-tension-wire box. The house, of recent construction, was built in classical colonial style: no stairway, a terrace, roof of corrugated sheet metal, situated in the middle of a small plot of land.

The prisoners were led from the cars and locked in the main room of the house. Policemen from Pius Sapwe's force took positions at the crossroad and set up a road-block on the asphalt road leading to the airport and on the road that led to Elizabethville. The Katangese police, commanded by the European officers mentioned above, guarded the interior of the house and its environs. All belonged to ethnic groups faithful to the Katangese rulers Lunda and Bayeke.

The Belgian Consulate alluded to this situation in a cable to Brussels on January 18, in which it was stated that "Lumumba was placed in a very well-guarded residence."

Ministerial Palavers

After the arrival of the prisoners, just as night was falling, President Tshombe held a meeting of the inner cabinet at his house. Evariste Kimba was present, as well as Joseph Kiwele, Jean-Baptiste Kibwe, and Lucas Samalenge.* They were later joined by Godefroid Munongo, who had supervised the operation at the airport. A long discussion began: what should be done with the prisoners?

No written account exists, to our knowledge, of the ministerial meeting. What filtered out of it was the fact that certain members wanted a quick judgment so that the prisoners could be executed without waiting; others wanted to retain them as hostages and send them to prison in Jadotville, with a view toward possible negotiation with the UN. It was apparently also suggested that they be sent back the next day to Leopoldville.

The tone of the meeting then became more and more lively; alcoholic beverages were generously consumed. Finally the council seems to have decided to send the prisoners to a "safer" place in Bunkeya—the home of the great chief Antoine Mwenda-Munongo,* a relative of the Minister of the Interior. Apparently a messenger—Godefroid Munongo, to be precise—was then sent to the Katangese guard to tell them of the decision. During this time the European circle close to the Katangese government was quite restless.

121

The question of which Katangese ministers saw the prisoners after their arrival and their imprisonment is not clear. For example, did Moise Tshombe see Lumumba?

According to his statements to Berendsen in January, 1961, Tshombe saw the prisoners during the evening of the seventeenth; they were, he said "in a sad state" and Lumumba, "whose face was swollen," asked for protection "in a pathetic way."

In January, 1964, however, Tshombe maintained the contrary: that he had had no contact with the prisoners. Apropos of his declaration to Berendsen, he said, "That day I was hiding the truth" and he swore that no one was able to speak with Lumumba, who "was, in any case, unconscious" upon his arrival. However, when he was in Madrid, Tshombe confided to a witness who may be trusted that he went to the place of detention at 9 P.M. and saw Lumumba "who was already at his last gasp." He also said that he prevented a Lunda guard from hitting him with the butt of a rifle. "I had tears in my eyes when I left the room," he declared to this witness. "I am persuaded that Lumumba died before my eyes."

What about the other ministers?

It has been affirmed that Kibwe and some other ministers, all of them drunk, went to the place of detention to enjoy the spectacle of their conquered enemy. During the night of January 17–18, Secretary of State for Information Lucas Samalenge, who has since died under suspicious circumstances, bragged in a bar that he had kicked Patrice Lumumba's dead body, and on January 18 he announced the death of the prisoners to his close collaborators, notably the journalist Daff.

This action caused Tshombe to summon Samalenge to his office for a long conversation and also perhaps to be put under arrest. Furthermore, the information bulletin No. 92 of the State of Katanga (January 19, 1961), notes in its Top Secret section that "the man named Daff, agent for the Minister of Information, declared in a public place in the city that Lumumba had already been liquidated through the services of the Katangese Sûreté.

What about Munongo? Even if we cannot prove that he was at the Browez house at the time of Lumumba's death, the decision to transfer Lumumba to Bunkeya, and the order given Munongo by the inner cabinet to inform the guards of their decision, both imply that the Minister of the Interior did in fact go to the place of detention during the evening.

ETAT du KATANGA.

XXXXXXXXXXX

Certificat de Décès
_____

Je soussigné G.Pieters

Médecin du Gouvernement Katangais

certifie que le nommé (nom. prénoms)

LUMUMBA Patrice

sexe masculin

âge 36 ens

est décédé à en brousse

au Katanga

Le Médecin.

14 février 1961

ETAT DU KATANGA
MINISTERE DE L'INTERIEUR

An Order for Execution?

Many different tales of the death of the prisoners have been circulated. But first of all we must try to elucidate this question: what possibility is there of the existence of a formal order to kill Lumumba and his companions? That is, were the prisoners killed under orders? If so, whose orders? Or did they die as a result of the blows they received? Or, even further, because of the criminal initiative of someone acting without orders?

Up until recently, it was generally admitted that there was no document in existence which might settle this question. On June 13, 1965, the weekly newspaper *Jeune Afrique* published what it called the "proof" of the direct and personal responsibility of Tshombe in the order for the execution of the prisoners. The text in question is in the form of a cabinet order signed by Tshombe, dated from Kolwezi on January 17, 1961, and addressed to Gat and "to the European officers of the First M.P. Company presently on a mission at Kolwezi," enjoining the latter to take charge of the three prisoners and execute them "without delay in the interests of the state."

The authenticity of this document is, to say the least, questionable. An expert in Katangese problems, present in Elizabethville at the time of the events, notes the following:

1. The First Company of the police was never stationed

125

in Kolwezi and its headquarters were always at Camp Massart in Elizabethville.

2. Captain Gat was in Elizabethville at that time and thus there was no reason to date the order Kolwezi.

3. The use of the expression "European officers" is hard to understand because, at that time, the entire officer staff was European. The definition is superfluous.

4. This "document" is supposed to have been found after four years, in Belgium, under unknown circumstances and in an undefined place.

5. Tshombe, also being in Elizabethville, had no reason to date the document Kolwezi.

6. Documents of the Katangese presidency, including orders of the mission, generally carried the seal of the President of the State of Katanga; the documents of January, 1963, at the time of the end of the secession, are the only exceptions to this rule. (We must remember that it was at Kolwezi that the secession came to an end.)

7. A group of men sympathetic to the secessionist regime took possession of the mission's blank forms at the time of the fall of the regime in December, 1962–January, 1963; the forms, which were meant to serve as compensation forms for the missions, could have either been lost or deliberately withheld.

8. Furthermore, the date of January 17 leads one to believe that Elizabethville was aware of the exact day of arrival of the prisoners.

We can add to the above the following remarks: It is rather improbable that on January 17, 1961, Elizabethville knew that Mr. Okito and Mr. Mpolo were with Patrice Lumumba in the DC-4. Besides, it is hard to believe that Tshombe, even if he were an advocate of the liquidation of the prisoners, and was informed of their presence, would have personally signed such a compromising document. It is also hard to imagine that Captain Gat would be so negligent as to lose this order or so indiscreet as to entrust it to a third party. Furthermore, it is also hard to understand why, if this order had been written, the Katangese cabinet would have had such long discussions on the evening of the seventeenth about the fate of the prisoners.

For certain people involved in the secession, the existence and disclosure of this document would have been a way of settling accounts between mercenaries and the Belgian officers of the Katangese police. In order to explain the existence and the possession of the order by a third party, those who circulated it after having proposed to sell it to anti-Tshombist circles offered the following explanation: Captain Gat presumably would have demanded that he be covered one hundred per cent for this risky operation. Fearing, furthermore, that they [the secessionists], judging him to be either too compromised or compromising, would attempt to eliminate him, he may have entrusted a copy of the document, or even the document itself, to one of his friends. We must recall that in 1964–65, ex-mercenaries of the Katangese police hardly hid their hostility to Tshombe. They had not, they said, received their back pay and indemnities due them for services rendered to the State of Katanga, while the officers received thousands as a price for their silence. At this time, Belgian newspapers of the extreme right[17] even alluded to an attempt, by ex-mercenaries of Katanga, to recruit European volunteers to join Christophe Gbenye's and G. Soumialot's Armée Populaire de Libération (Popular Liberation Army).

To all appearances, the published document must have

---

[17] See, for example, *Jeune Europe*, number 211.

been forged or written *after the fact,* based on a blank form signed by Mr. Tshombe and entrusted to certain members of the Katangese police at the crucial moments of secession.

Thus, no document permits us to definitely affirm the existence of an order for execution emanating from an authority.

Death

There have been many different versions of the circumstances of Lumumba's death in circulation. They come from people who were involved in the affair either immediately or from a distance, from the UN Commission of Inquiry, and from journalists and editors who attempted to put the facts together. We have discovered versions which fall into four groups:

1. Those versions which have been proven false (Munongo and Duchemin versions).

2. Those which directly implicate Minister of the Interior Godefroid Munongo (Van Lierde, Tournaire, *Auto-Journal*, De Vos, *Révolution Africaine*).

2a. Those which directly incriminate the Katangese and Congolese authorities (a witness for the UN Commission of Inquiry and Van den Heuvel).

3. The version which denies all Katangese responsibility (Moise Tshombe).

4. Those which impute the crime to Europeans, either acting under orders from, or independent of, Katangese authorities (Nkrumah, *Jeune Afrique*, three witnesses heard by the UN Commission).

It should be noted that besides the name Gat, mention is made several times of a certain Ruys, of whom we could find no trace. Also mentioned is a certain Huyghe, an ex-Belgian colonial who had become the adviser to the

Katangese Minister of Defense. Mr. Huyghe, when interrogated, denied the statements made concerning him and we must admit that our investigation has led us to the same conclusion—that is, that he was not directly linked to the death of the prisoners.

To understand why some people felt free to say they were involved in the death of Lumumba, we must recall the climate at the time in Elizabethville as well as in Leopoldville. Certain people were to consider such involvement an "honor" at that time and to brag, even to the point of excess, about having contributed to the liquidation of the prisoners. Later, with a better sense of the repercussions of the affair, they denied the allegations and the accusations made against them. Following are some of the versions concerning the death of Lumumba and his companions:

1. Kwame Nkrumah, former president of Ghana, in a statement to Reuters Agency (February 19, 1961):

Mr. Lumumba and his two lieutenants received the order to leave their Katangese prison on January 18 and they were told to pray. While they were kneeling, a Belgian officer ordered an African to fire at them. The two lieutenants were executed but the soldier lowered his rifle when he came to Lumumba, and refused to fire. The Belgian then reached for his revolver and killed Lumumba.

2. Gaston Bunnens, Belgian journalist, in *Germinal* (March 8, 1963):

The Belgian officers [who were in the service of the State of Katanga] told me the following:

"The [Katangese] ministers were overcome by a veritable madness. It was impossible to reason with them.

But President Tshombe is not responsible for what happened. It happened in his absence.

"But I have seen photos taken by UN officers showing Tshombe examining Lumumba, who is kneeling before him.

"Yes, the President went to see Lumumba, then he called a cabinet meeting to decide whether the former prime minister would be brought to trial. In the meantime, he was to be imprisoned in Bunkeya, Munongo's native village. But after the meeting the ministers celebrated the capture of their enemy. They drank as if their stomachs were bottomless! And on the same evening, at 11 o'clock, Munongo and Kibwe went to the place of detention and called the prisoners names and insulted them. The latter, having arrived in a pitiable state, were entirely unconscious. It is then that Munongo and Kibwe, on the outer limits of their drunkenness, killed Lumumba, working him over before making Mpolo and Okito undergo the same fate."

3. Francis Monheim, Belgian journalist, in *Mobutu, l'homme seul* (Editions Actuelles, Brussels, 1962) :

When Lumumba arrived in Elizabethville, he had not yet been seriously maltreated; that, at least, is the impression that a member of the Board of Commissioners, who happened to be at Elizabethville airport, received from a brief conversation he had with the prisoner.

Minister Munongo "welcomed" the prisoners and the hideous execution took place soon thereafter.

Munongo had the men led away to a vacant lot near the airport. A terrible argument ensued between him and Lumumba, in which Lumumba recovered his impetuosity and fire. Munongo doubtlessly wanted to pronounce an indictment of Lumumba, but it was Lumumba who accused *him*. Lumumba knew he was lost; thus, for the last time, he hurled all his anger, his hatred, and his indignation in the face of the minister who had "sold out to the Belgians."

And, speaking to the soldiers who struck him because he had "insulted the minister," Lumumba said simply with a smile: "Emery's in true form."

There was a burst of gunfire. Patrice Lumumba fell. Behind him in the firing line, Okito was crying like a little boy, while Mpolo knelt down in prayer. The three of them were killed.

4. Helene Tournaire and Robert Bouteaud, French writer-reporters, in *Livre Noir du Congo* (Librairie Académique Perrin, Paris, 1963) :

. . . Without any intervention on the part of the *casques bleus*, the convoy left through a hole in the airport fence.

Munongo was waiting several kilometers away. They were surrounded by the unchanging savannah, with its red dusty dirt and its termite hills higher than trees. Patrice Lumumba was even redder than the earth on the road. His bandage was torn off and the sun wounded what remained of his eyes. Godefroid Munongo approached him. French was their only language in common. Munongo used it, not to hurl insults, not to mock, but to make an allusion to ancient beliefs:

"Do you still think you're invulnerable?"

Munongo pulled a bayonet out of a state policeman's belt. He leaned over Lumumba. Slowly, steadily, the bayonet was buried between his ribs. We do not understand, and no one will ever be able to explain to us, the ritual involved in this murder. The slowness of the gesture piercing the heart of the enemy is perhaps only a refined ferociousness. We do not believe so. The European mercenaries (Belgians, and an Englishman, Russell-Cargill) who had met in this spot and were drinking to "celebrate" the arrival of Lumumba, had been warned of this assassination and were waiting for it, but could not bear the sight of it. Colonel Huyghe drew his revolver and, aiming for the head, pulled the trigger. That's called the coup de grâce. Captain Gat also had his revolver in his hand.

5. F. Bernier, C. Lamic, F. Vic, French reporters, in *Auto-Journal* (April 6, 1961):

Last January 17, a few minutes before 5 P.M., a DC-4 landed at the airport in Elizabethville. . . . The field and its approaches were guarded by soldiers of the military police. These soldiers were black. Most of them were members of the First Company, the only one that remained faithful and opposed the riot in Elizabethville in July, 1960. Some of their officers were white. They were lent as part of Belgian technical aid to the Free State of Katanga. There were, among others, Captain Gat and Lieutenant Grandelet, who was wounded during the course of one of the above-mentioned riots. . . .

. . . It was Munongo who had won. He struck the ex-President of the Council violently. Okito had fallen to his feet and was praying. Mpolo accused his chief: "It's because of you that we are here."

Dignified, but exhausted, Lumumba faced his adversaries: "I know that you are going to kill me."

"Oh, come now!" said Munongo.

A captain who was about a yard behind the former prime minister of the Congo fired point blank several times. Lumumba fell. He was dead. Mpolo and Okito were executed several minutes later. No witnesses must remain.

On January 18, in the native *Cité* of Elizabethville, the police quietly and gently locked up the Minister of Intelligence, Mr. Samalenge; drunk, he recounted the scene to all who wanted to hear it.

This is the truth about the Lumumba affair.

6. In a Belgian publication, *Le Dossier du Mois* (du Ponant, ed., Brussels, No. 4–5, April–May, 1964):

Waiting impatiently in the control tower was Munongo, the ferocious Minister of the Interior of the Katangese government. At that time he said to the European officer who was at his side, "This time, they will not get away!" . . .

A team of eight European officers and warrant officers was named by the Katangese authorities. The chief of this commando was Captain G.; his assistant is Lieutenant M. Among them were also Second Lieutenant L. and Sergeant Major R.

It was in this small building, during the night of the seventeenth to the eighteenth of January that the three prisoners were shot with a short 9 mm. The officers mentioned are not to be blamed; they were executing orders, as doubtless it was their duty to do.

Besides, these orders were only too clear; it is of course difficult to say whether the Katangese ministers were present at the time of the execution, but it is none the less certain that they came several times to see the prisoners, Tshombe among them.

7. Pierre De Vos, Belgian journalist, in *Vie et mort de Lumumba* (Calmann-Lévy, ed., Paris, 1961) :

Once more—as on July 12, 1960, when he refused to let the plane which was carrying Kasavubu and Lumumba, pilgrims of Congolese unity, land at Luano—the Minister of the Interior, Godefroid Munongo, was in the control tower. But that day he would himself welcome the head of the central government. . . .

And it was the end—the cries: "He mustn't dirty Katangese soil," and then the sad murder. Did Munongo personally assign himself this task? We say yes, and we also note that he had expressed this intention on several different occasions. In the truck, traveling through the brush, between the termite hills, the black henchman, with the sardonic smile on his face that we can so easily imagine, kept asking Lumumba:

"So, are you still invulnerable? Do you still spit bullets?"

Then he shoved a bayonet into his chest. Slowly. Steadily. A white man gave the coup de grâce.

8. Jean Van Lierde, Belgian journalist, in *La pensée politique de Lumumba* (Présence Africaine, Paris, 1963) :

Just as on July 12, 1960, the sinister Munongo, Katangese Minister of the Interior, was at the airport. . . .
. . . On that day, he had refused to let the plane carrying Kasavubu and Lumumba land. He was cynically triumphant now : he was finally going to be able to put an end to the extraordinary life of the Congolese leader who symbolized the authentic African revolution and the death throes of imperialism.

The trucks, jeeps, and armored cars left Luano airport immediately, escaping from the UN patrols, and disappeared into the night.

A mile or so from there, in a secluded house still under construction, Munongo and some Belgian officers and some Katangese soldiers executed Mpolo and Okito. While his comrades, kneeling and praying to God, fell in a hail of bullets, Patrice Lumumba, standing, heroically looked steadily at the filthy brute who would pierce him with a bayonet before the bullets finished the task.

The prime minister of the first government of the Republic of the Congo is dead.

9. Jacques Duchemin, French adviser in the Congo, in *Notre guerre au Katanga* (Pensée Moderne, Paris, 1963) :

In the meantime, Lumumba was imprisoned in the apartment of the director of the Jadotville prison. The hatred of Minister of Interior Munongo, who was urged on by the chief of the cabinet, the Belgian Tignée and Major Carlos Huyghe, constituted a threat for Lumumba which will soon become explicit. While waiting, he went on a hunger strike. . . .

In Jadotville, Lumumba and his two companions were the responsibility of the governor of Kolwezi, Veston Muteba. He was a strapping young man, an ex-garage manager, who was known for his eccentricities. . . .

On February 6, at 6:30 P.M., Katangese policemen entered the dining room; Lumumba stood up and understood all when he saw their faces. He cried, "You don't have the right!"

He was killed, along with the two others because all three of them were together, by bursts of pistol fire which were so wild that several policemen wounded each other. Munongo arrived soon thereafter and began to dance with joy; then Tshombe arrived. The latter cried, knelt down and began to pray, hurling insults at the police and saying that that was not what he had wanted.

10. In an Algerian publication, *Révolution Africaine* (No. 155, January 15–21, 1966) :

Even though there are several versions of the assassination of Lumumba, the same names come up each time: Tshombe; Munongo; Kibwe; the Belgian mercenaries Julien Gat, Michel, Léva, Rouchefort, Huyghe. . . .

Having arrived on January 17, 1961, in Elizabethville at 6 P.M., Lumumba and his companions were "taken charge of" by Godefroid Munongo at Luano Airport in Elizabethville. . . .

Lumumba and his companions were taken to a small, isolated house. A grave had already been dug in the surrounding savannah. According to the statements of the late Lucas Samalenge, Tshombe; Kibwe, the vice-president of Katanga; Munongo; Kitenge, the Minister of Public Works; Pius Sapwe, the chief of the Katangese police, and Samalenge himself arrived that night at the place of Lumumba's martyrdom. Some Belgian mercenaries, Julien Gat, Michel, Léva, and Rouchefort were there with some Katangese state police, who were to be the grave diggers.

Tshombe then demanded that Lumumba "ask forgiveness for all his bad actions against Katanga," and also that he recognize, in writing, "the independence of Katanga." Lumumba flatly refused! He was then savagely beaten by Kibwe and Munongo. The latter pierced his chest with a bayonet. The mercenaries fired and Captain Gat finished him off. Maurice Mpolo and Joseph Okito were killed without ceremony. And under the guise of a secret oath, the white mercenaries each dipped his hand in Lumumba's blood. It was the birth of the "group of the red hand," well known by all the mercenaries who were close friends of Tshombe's.

11. In an African publication *Jeune Afrique* (June 15, 1965) :

The plane carrying Patrice Lumumba and his companions was preparing to land. Mr. Munongo and Captain Protin left the control tower for the landing strip. There they found the corpulent and jolly Pius Sapwe, commissioner of the Katangese police, and the officers of the First Company who were recalled that same morning from Kolwezi. The commander of this company was Captain Julien Gat, his assistant, First Lieutenant Michel. Second Lieutenant Roger Léva was charged with the administration of this company. . . . Sergeant Major Rouchefort was head of a squad of this company. . . .

At nightfall, the Katangese soldiers went off duty, except for eight men, the officers of the First Company of the police who stayed in the house with Lumumba and his companions. Who came to join them?

Jeune Afrique then states that it is not in a position to confirm or deny any of the testimony about the presence of the Katangese ministers, but adds:

There is however one element about which all our information agrees: this is that it was one of the eight men who were in the house (that is, the Belgian mer-

cenaries Gat, Michel, Léva, Rouchefort and the four
others whose names we were not able to ascertain) who
carried out Tshombe's orders. . . . Lumumba, Okito,
Mpolo were killed one after the other in cold blood, with
the help of a short 9 mm. It is unlikely, as was first stated,
that Lumumba was killed first, but, on the contrary, last.
The name most often cited, each time Lumumba's death
is discussed, is Julien Gat.

12. Remy Van Den Heuvel, Belgian colonial in Katanga, in *De Post* (Antwerp, no. 888, March 13, 1966) :

I categorically affirm—and I am ready to repeat this
under oath if necessary—that Pius Sapwe personally
recounted to me on January 18, 1961, how he had, at
the request of Tshombe and Munongo, finished off
Lumumba with a single shot from his revolver. This
happened during the night of January 17, quite soon
after the "delivery" of the Lumumba-package to the
Katangese, in an unoccupied house belonging to Sabena
personnel situated near the airport in Elizabethville.
    The final phase of the drama also took place near there.
Why, in any case, should they have gone any farther?
Lumumba was buried in a place which is called in Elizabethville "l'Ancienne Plaine," the old abandoned airport, a no man's land, deserted and invaded by weeds, a
fitting setting for this end.

13. Moise Tshombe, former president of Katanga, in
Pourquoi pas? (January 31, 1964; declaration to Pierre
Davister) :

"Covered with blows from their guards, the six colossal
Baluba of M. Kazadi's escort and the three prisoners
were transported to an empty house in the quarter,
known as the 'Sabena Quarter' because that company's
agents live there. The residence, let us emphasize, was not
being lived in. Night fell."

"Is it therefore in this house that the crime took place?"

"What crime? There was no crime. The truth is both simpler and less sensational: the prisoners were dying."

"All three?"

"All three."

"But people have said that Godefroid Munongo . . ."

"That's false. Munongo was as worried as I was about the alarming state of the captives."

"Did you see them in the house they were transferred to?"

"No." . . .

"If you didn't see the prisoners in the house, what proves to you then that Munongo wasn't lying and that there was no crime?"

"Because there was a witness in that house, a man whom I have complete confidence in, and who has never lied to me and never will."

"Which witness?"

"Pius Sapwe, the Commissioner of Police of Elizabethville."

Lumumba, Okito, and Mpolo were dying; a medical examination confirmed the evidence: a miracle would have been needed to save them. This miracle, however, had no chance of happening in the house where the three men were hidden.

Lumumba had an internal hemorrhage, a perforated stomach, broken ribs. Okito had a fractured skull which was visible to the naked eye. Mpolo was in a sort of coma, but suffered every so often from strange convulsions. Such serious wounds would require surgery in a well-equipped hospital. Therefore Tshombe would have had to order a new transfer.

At this point in the narrative, the ex-president hesitated, then confided to me:

"At that point," he said, "I acted like Pontius Pilate. I didn't dare order this transfer, and I admit it, I was panicked."

"Could they have still been saved?"

"Medical opinion, and there was a medical opinion,

was categorical: they had only a few hours to live. This diagnosis was too optimistic even so. . . ."

14. Godefroid Munongo, former Minister of the Interior of Katanga, in a press conference on February 13, 1961:

Yesterday, during the evening, a Katangese man of the region of Kolwezi (I will not be more precise) came to see me at my private residence to announce that Lumumba, Okito, and Mpolo had been murdered yesterday morning by the inhabitants of a small village situated quite some distance from the spot where their car had been found— so far in fact that we still wonder how the three fugitives were able to get there.

This morning we went to the spot by airplane. Minister Kibwe, Minister Kitenge, and myself were able to identify the three dead men.

We were accompanied by a doctor who was able to write out a death certificate, if in fact we did find Lumumba, Okito, and Mpolo.

They were identified beyond all possible doubt and their death was confirmed. The corpses were immediately buried in a spot we will not let be known, if only to avoid eventual pilgrimages.

Neither will we reveal the name of the village which finally put an end to these sad exploits of Lumumba and his accomplices. In fact, we do not want these Katangese, whose tribe will not be mentioned, to be the object of eventual reprisals by Lumumbists. . . .

15. Testimony gathered by the UN Commission of Inquiry: A first anonymous witness furnished at the same time a version of the death, and testimony concerning the fate of the corpses. The Commission does not state whether this is a direct eyewitness or simply a person reporting rumors.

When the plane landed at Elizabethville, Mr. Lumumba and his companions were transferred to a truck and led a mile or so away from the airport. Mr. Munongo, who awaited his arrival, came toward Mr. Lumumba and, after having made some remarks, took the bayonet of a rifle belonging to one of the soldiers and buried it in Mr. Lumumba's chest. While Mr. Lumumba lay dying, a certain Captain Ruys, a mercenary of Belgian origin serving in the Katangese army, put an end to his sufferings by lodging a bullet in his head. Captain Ruys' gesture, the witness thought, came from purely humanitarian feelings. When Mr. Tshombe learned of the death of Mr. Lumumba, he flew into a great rage, again according to the witness. But, having to face a *fait accompli,* he had to imagine a way to change public opinion. He had Mr. Lumumba's body carried off in an ice chest belonging to the laboratories of the Union Minière du Haut-Katanga. Then the body was plunged into formaldehyde.

15a. The second version reported by the UN Commission directly implicates a Belgian colonial who had become an administrator in the secretariat of the Katangese state in the Defense Ministry.

A British mercenary, captured by the UN in Katanga and evacuated from the Congo according to Paragraph A-2 of the Security Council resolution on February 21, 1961, spontaneously gave information to the chief of the Military Intelligence Services of the UN before taking the plane to Brazzaville to go to Johannesburg. When he was in Johannesburg on leave from his service in the Katangese police, he learned from his wife that Mr. Russell-Cargill had told her that Mr. Lumumba and his two companions had been killed by the Belgian colonel Huyghe. This British mercenary had later met Colonel Huyghe and asked him if that were true. Colonel Huyghe admitted that he really had killed Mr. Lumumba and his two companions with the aid of a certain Captain Gat, another Belgian mercenary, and some other European volunteers serving in the Katangese police near Elizabethville in the garden of a villa where several men had gone to drink in order to "celebrate" the arrival of Mr. Lu-

mumba and his companions. The British mercenary added
that Mr. Tshombe, Mr. Munongo, and several other ministers were present at the time of the assassination, and
that Mr. Russell-Cargill was also there. He was not able
to indicate the exact date of the events, but he assumed
that they took place the day of the arrival of the prisoners
in Elizabethville. Colonel Huyghe had said that the assassination was prepared in advance. The corpses had
been taken out of the city, but no detail was given concerning the spot to which they were transported and the
methods used to get rid of the bodies.

The British mercenary said, moreover, that Colonel
Huyghe seemed to be very agitated and that since then
he had consulted a psychiatrist. He always carried a revolver with him and had grenades close at hand in his
bedroom to defend himself against possible arrest.

15b. The facts contained in the above declaration have
been confirmed in their broad outline by another British
mercenary who testified before the Commission. Among
other things, he said:

I would not be able to repeat for you word by word
what we said in the course of this conversation; we had,
I remind you, drunk quite a lot, but I still have clearly in
mind the answers he gave me. For example, I asked
Huyghe: "Is the story published in the press, according
to which Lumumba escaped in a car, correct? If so, it's
really a ridiculous thing to leave a car in front of the
door so that the prisoners can escape, unless all that was
organized in advance."

At this juncture, Huyghe began to speak and told me
the story, speaking in the first person. He told me that
he was present at the execution of Lumumba. I tried to
make him say more, and to begin with he added that
some soldiers of the state of Katanga were present at the
farm where Lumumba and his two companions were detained. A Katangese minister, he told me, was also present; I can't say whether it was Munongo or Kibwe, but I

know that it was a minister of prime importance. He
continued by saying that Lumumba's two companions
were led into a room and invited to pray for their lives,
and while they were kneeling, they were killed by a shot
in the nape of the neck.

He then told me that Lumumba was in turn led into the
room where he himself [Huyghe] killed him with a shot
from a revolver. Apropos of the death of Lumumba,
Huyghe told me that when Lumumba was led into the
room, he began to scream, to ask for pity, and to beg
that his life be saved. He turned successively to each of
the persons present, promising them all the rewards
they wanted if they would save him. Huyghe, continuing
his story, told me: "Then I told him: 'Pray, you bastard'
(please excuse the expression, but those were his exact
words). 'You had no pity whatsoever for the women,
the children, and even the nuns of your own faith. The
hour has come for you to pray.' "

According to Huyghe, Lumumba then rolled on the
floor, crying and asking for pity, and it is at that moment,
Huyghe told me, that "I killed him while he was rolling
on the floor." "Christ, it isn't possible, Charles." And he
said, "Yes, Roddy, it is true." But I must emphasize here
that, as I told your legal counsel in Leopoldville, we had
both been drinking that night and it is not at all impossible that Huyghe was just bragging. However, I don't
consider him incapable of having actually done what he
told me he did that night.

15c. Finally, the Commission heard the testimony of an
official high up in the government of the province of
Katanga, a close collaborator of Tshombe. This witness
declared:

According to what I heard on Tuesday evening, certain
ministers of the Katangese government supposedly came
to visit Mr. Lumumba; they became somewhat excited
about him and, at a certain moment, one of the ministers
violently struck Mr. Lumumba, who then fell on a bidet

which was apparently in the room. He remained unconscious and was apparently killed by this blow. I don't
know whether he had already been struck before. According to what I have been told, he had already been
manhandled in the airplane.

Asked to give an explanation of the fate reserved for
Lumumba's companions, the witness declared:

Rumors say that they were also killed, but as a conse-
quence of the accident which took place when the Prime
Minister was ill-treated.

Asked then to give precise details about the place where
the events took place, the witness affirmed:

In several communications which I heard in the meetings, they spoke of a hotel which was quite near the airport. In fact it was a sort of riding club. . . . It's a new
establishment which I have never frequented. I spoke of
a hotel, but it is not exactly a hotel. It's rather a public
house which also serves as a place for horsemen to meet.
I have never personally been there. I don't know whether
it has a name. I don't think so.

15d. Conclusions of the UN Commission of Inquiry:

. . . The Commission considers the following version
true as far as the essential points go: the account according to which the prisoners were killed on January
17, 1961, after their arrival, in a villa near Elizabethville
and very probably under the eyes of certain members
of the government of the province of Katanga, notably
Tshombe, Munongo, and Kibwe, and that the story of an
escape was entirely invented.

Clues point heavily to a certain Colonel Huyghe, a Belgian mercenary, who is most likely the real murderer of
Mr. Lumumba and who probably carried out his crime
according to a premeditated plan with the help of a cer-

tain Captain Gat, another Belgian mercenary. As for Okito and Mpolo, it is not clear who in fact killed them, but indications are that they were killed at the same time as Mr. Lumumba.

Without being able to confirm this, the Commission believes that a shot was fired by Captain Ruys at Mr. Lumumba to end the latter's suffering, and that the theory that Mr. Lumumba's body was placed in a refrigerator belonging to the laboratories of Union Minière du Haut-Katanga . . . should be accepted with grave reservations. However, the Commission wishes to note, relative to this question, that the points listed above should, in any case, not be disregarded in all subsequent inquiries.

Other versions are in circulation, but they all have this in common: each version totally exonerates the circle of people which tells it. This much is certain: that the prisoners—received by Minister Munongo and confided to the care of guards acting under Munongo's orders—died during the evening of January 17 or the night of the seventeenth or the eighteenth on Katangese soil. We can believe that the prisoners had been struck or wounded, and that a finishing blow was given to Lumumba by means of a 9 mm. P.G., a gun not carried by the ordinary Katangese police. Did Lumumba's companions die before him, or, on the contrary, were they killed so that some day they would not be able to serve as witnesses? The most likely version is the second. In Katangese circles, it is generally admitted that Lumumba died without asking for pity from his adversaries and his guards. As far as we can establish, the prisoners died in the house where they were imprisoned after their arrival.

When the prisoners were already dead, Brussels received a telex message from its representative in Elizabethville (January 18, 1961), affirming that it was the intention of Katangese authorities to transfer Lumumba "immediately to a safe place . . . to treat him properly and even . . . to make him participate at the Round Table in the role of accused."

What Became of
the Bodies?

There have also been several differing versions in circulation about the fate of the corpses: that they were buried after a short time; that they were tied up, weighted, and thrown into an abandoned well belonging to the Union Minière; that they were put in sulfuric acid and formaldehyde, supplied by a mining company, during the night of January 17–18; or else stored for a while in an ice chest belonging to a local European company (the Elakat or the Union Minière) so that they might be produced if circumstances demanded it. We record some of the opinions below.

1. Pierre De Vos, Belgian journalist, in *Vie et mort de Lumumba* (Calmann-Lévy, ed., Paris, 1961):

Then began a rather horrible and extraordinary tragicomedy, played out in great secret. When Moise Tshombe learned of the torture and death of Patrice Lumumba, he weighed the consequences and was frightened, because this man, in his heart of hearts, is a moderate. The consequences could have been fateful, bringing repercussions not only against the whites who are still quite numerous in the provinces run by Mr. Gizenga, but also against the black anti-Lumumbists; they might also cause an invasion of Katanga by the African countries which have always

147

supported Lumumba despite his excesses. Tshombe gave
his orders: the news would be kept secret for several
weeks in order to see how the situation evolved. But what
should be done with a corpse in a tropical climate that
rots everything it touches? The sinister small truck in
which the dead leader had been laid arrived at nightfall
in front of the laboratories of an important mining company. The Belgian directors were there. They agreed to
let the body be placed in an ice chest. Several days later,
in order to preserve it better, it was put in a bath of
formaldehyde; thus it could be shown when a plausible
explanation had been found.

2. The Union Minière du Haut-Katanga in a communiqué published in *Le Soir* (Brussels, June 25, 1961):

Certain information has recently been circulated about
the role that might have been played, at the time of Patrice Lumumba's death, by directors or agents of a mining company in Elizabethville.

Furthermore, special mention has been made of the
Union Minière, which responded immediately with a
formal denial.

In view of the rumors which continue to be published,
the Union Minière again confirms this denial: neither its
directors, nor its agents, nor its equipment played any
role whatsoever in this affair.

2a. Reply of the Union Minière du Haut-Katanga to
the newspaper *Le Peuple* (June 16, 1961):

Under the title: "The ice chest that contains the corpse
of Lumumba belongs to the Union Minière!" you write:
"Information having been gathered from very good
sources [*sic*], we are in a position to state that these ice
chests belong to the Union Minière du Haut-Katanga."
And you add that Belgian opinion awaits our explanation
with interest.

Our explanation is as short as it is clear: there is not

one true word in your odious accusations and if, as you say, "Belgian opinion" awaits our explanations with interest, it also waits for you to reveal the trustworthy sources [sic] you used in order to verify, on the one hand, the seriousness with which your newspaper fills its role as a provider of information and, on the other hand, the seriousness which can be accorded the people who inform you.

3. *De Nieuwe Gazet* published an interview by one of its editors with Captain Gat, Belgian officer of the Katangese State Police, who was at the head of the troops charged with the surveillance of Lumumba after his transfer to Katanga. Interviewed on June 12, 1961, in the *Cité* and asked about a version published by a Belgian journalist in a French weekly—according to which the corpse of the former prime minister was preserved in an ice chest after January 17—Captain Gat termed this version completely imaginary. He himself was in charge of several units that day and he was not at the spot where the events took place.

After having repeated that it was entirely an invention, Captain Gat refused to give further details. "The truth will come out in the future and it is not my duty to give an official version of the events," he added.

4. Gaston Bunnens, Belgian journalist writing in *Germinal* (March 8, 1963) interrogated a European officer who belonged to the headquarters of the Katangese police during secession:

"And what about the ice chests belonging to 'the important mining company,' where according to our sources the bodies were put for the trumped-up escape?

"That is pure invention! For the simple reason that on the night of January 17 there were no longer any corpses!

The mining company simply supplied us with the sulfuric acid that we asked for. The corpses were entirely dissolved. There was nothing left of them."

5. *Le Dossier du Mois*, Belgian publication (Editions du Ponant, Brussels, Nos. 4–5, April–May, 1964):

Basing ourselves on current information, we have concluded that the corpses of the three men were buried immediately not far from the small house. But dogs came and scratched over this freshly turned earth. The next day, on January 19, in the presence of the Commissioner of Police of Elizabethville, the bodies were uncovered. They were tied up and weighted down, and then thrown into the well of the *Étoile* mine, an abandoned mine belonging to the Union Minière. This well has a depth of nearly 120 feet; the bodies, or what remains of them, are still there.

There is, however, another version of this story, and some of our informers strongly believed in it. According to them, the bodies were not buried, but were transported into the city and placed in ice chests belonging to the Elakat. Motive? Suddenly worried about the consequences of this liquidation, the Katangese leaders thus decided to preserve the bodies, should the need arise in the future, under more favorable circumstances, to "produce" them. It is with this in mind that, three weeks later, the scenario of the escape was enacted. However, facts did not require an exhibition of the corpses and they were then thrown into the *Étoile* mine (or, simply buried deeply in the bush, as some people assert).

And the supposed dissolution of the bodies in cisterns filled with sulfuric acid? Pure nonsense.

6. Moise Tshombe, former president of Katanga, in *Le Soir* (February 13, 1964):

The three bodies were buried the night of their death in a small cemetery situated on the Kasenga Road, near Ruashi Commune, in Elizabethville.

This secret burial will disappoint those who tell sensational stories. We had intended, in fact—and I say intended—to postdate in some way Patrice Lumumba's death and that of his companions, in order to gain time, time which was indispensable in finding a way to extricate ourselves from the impasse that Leopoldville has thrown us into. . . .

Afterwards, the demand for a transfer of the bodies (demand made by Lumumba's family), as well as the threat of the arrival of a Commission of Inquiry from the UN, frightened the leaders in Leopoldville, who feared that the discovery of the body would demonstrate their obvious culpability. This "disappearance" [of the bodies] took place, in fact, and it was Mr. Adoula who, advised by his close associates, decided on the method and its application. The bodies were uncovered and thrown into a bath of acid so that they would disappear forever.

Reality is doubtlessly simpler: the bodies were transported beyond the site of the massacre to the immediate area surrounding the Browez house by the men who had been guarding the prisoners. The earth was raked and smoothed over by machines provided by a company whose yards were close by.

No direct document or testimony concerning this act of the drama has been published. The officers of the guard were themselves excused from writing the usual mission report.

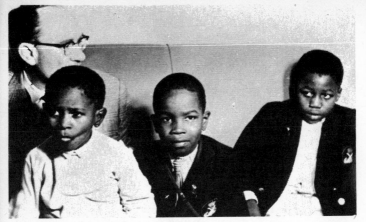

Lumumba's children: (from left to right) François, Patrice, and Juliana, in Cairo, November, 1960. —Belga

Lumumba's wife, Pauline, and their youngest son, Roland, a few days after Lumumba's death. —Associated Press *(Wide World Photos)*

After His Death

As soon as the announcement of the transfer of Lumumba to Elizabethville was made, African and Soviet protests were vehemently expressed in the UN. In Leopoldville, the UN Peace-Making Commission, which was interrogating provincial president Kamitatu that day, did not seem to be informed of the event.

Lumumba and his companions died during the night of January 17–18. On the afternoon of January 18, in Washington, the American Under Secretary of State for African Affairs summoned one of the Belgian representatives to tell him his thoughts about the transfer and the treatment that the prisoners were receiving. He insisted that Lumumba not be "liquidated" nor undergo bad treatment; such actions would result in renewed sympathies in Lumumba's favor in the moderate African countries.

The first tangible effect that the transfer of Lumumba had on the relations between authorities in Leopoldville and those in Katanga and South Kasai was an acceleration of the military negotiations with the view of creating a Leopoldville–Elizabethville–Bakwanga axis. On January 19, while an envoy of Abbé Youlou was in Elizabethville seeking financial aid for the presidential referendum, Congolese officers, assisted by Colonel Marlière, came to Katanga to discuss the possibility of a central authority and of an agreement on military cooperation.

On January 23, Victor Nendaka was also in Elizabethville; he arrived there by DC-4 at 10:40 A.M. and the same evening returned to Leopoldville on board a Boeing 707 at 7 P.M., accompanied by Mr. Delvaux and other delegates.

That day, January 23, Information Bulletin number 25 of the State of Katanga recorded rumors current in Jadotville which said that "Lumumba is said to have been executed by Congolese soldiers during his transfer to Elizabethville." Radio Katanga announced, then denied, the death of Mpolo.

A Belgian adviser to the Congolese Sûreté informed Brussels, also on January 23, that "in the first place, the transfer of Lumumba brought about an undeniable relaxation of tension in Leopoldville; the removal from Thysville and Luzumu prisons of other political prisoners is also envisaged. . . ."[18]

On January 27, the same Belgian agent noted the "indiscretions of Delvaux and Kazadi" which, he supposed, were the source of "the rumor [which] is beginning to circulate in Leopoldville stating that Lumumba was supposedly executed in Elizabethville," and, speaking to Brussels and the Belgian Consulate in Elizabethville, he added ". . . if Lumumba is still alive, I suggest you put an end to the rumors."

The next day, Godefroid Munongo, speaking to a delegation from South Kasai led by Albert Kalonji, and of which Jonas Mukamba was a member, confided that he did not want to fulfill the Mulopwe's wish of transferring Lumumba to Bakwanga: "It is an honor for us to kill

[18] This probably refers to the project for transfer (carried out on February 9, 1961) to Bakwanga of the Lumumbist leaders, who were then killed there in the most atrocious manner.

this man on Katangese soil," he supposedly declared at that time.

Beginning on January 20, in Stanleyville, threats of harsh reprisals against the Belgians were vehemently set forth in a telegram sent by B. Salumu, Commissioner of the district, to King Baudouin: "The disappearance of Lumumba from this world will be followed by that of thousands of Belgians living in our territory because it is Belgium which is at the root of all events in the Congo . . . we have the satisfaction of letting no Belgian live on our soil, including women and children." The UN—which was menaced with the withdrawal of contingents from the U.A.R., Morocco, and Guinea—issued appeals for calm, while Hammarskjöld asked Kasavubu and Tshombe to bring Lumumba back to Leopoldville.

On January 21, Justin Bomboko made a "report to the Council on the advisability and the conditions of the transfer of Mr. Lumumba to Elizabethville," according to the official record of the meeting.

In the beginning of February, first an American plan and then an Afro-Asian plan was presented to the UN, posing the problem of a fundamental reorganization of the armed forces in the Congo. A violent anti-UN reaction took place at the heart of the ANC and within the ranks of the authorities in Leopoldville and Elizabethville. The repeated demands made to President Kasavubu, Tshombe, and Nendaka by the UN Peace-Making Mission to see the prisoners were totally ignored. The UN soon adopted a tough resolution demanding the expulsion of European advisers and European mercenaries from the Congo.

While Abbé Youlou was receiving a triumphant reception in Katanga and the French Colonel Trinquier was be-

ing spoken of as the next commander of the Katangese
police, a provisional government was set up in Leopoldville with Joseph Ileo as president after the dissolution of
the Board of Commissioners General.

More and more rumors circulated about Lumumba's
death. It was at that time—on February 10—that
Munongo maintained that the prisoners had escaped. On
February 13, the Katangese minister recited the story,
entirely false, of the death of Lumumba and his two
companions.

At the UN, a violent campaign was launched by the
Soviet Union against Mr. Hammarskjöld. The same day,
the Lumumbist regime in Stanleyville was recognized
by Moscow and Cairo, soon followed by Belgrade,
Conakry, Rabat, Accra, Tirana, Havana, Warsaw, Buda-
pest, and Peking.

At the pre-Round Table conference in Leopoldville,
Ileo asked for a minute of silence for "the tragic death
of the head of the first government" and for the Congolese victims of the troubled situation. In Stanleyville,
Monseigneur Kinsch, the Roman Catholic bishop, celebrated a mass in the memory of Patrice Lumumba, and
General Lundula asked the crowd to be calm.

APPENDICES

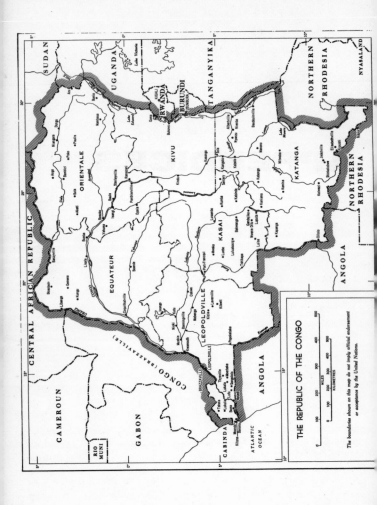

Map of the Republic of the Congo, 1962 — Courtesy: United Nations

A

Patrice Lumumba Speaks

Explanatory notes by Paul Roland, Disques Sonopresse, Rotterdam

[These transcribed] excerpts . . . were taken from speeches and statements [Lumumba] made in 1960 and early in 1961. They were recorded live, often under difficult technical conditions. [First is] a statement made by Lumumba to the "Amis de Présence Africaine" in Brussels in January, 1960:

Dear fellow citizens: This is Lumumba, the Prime Minister of the Republic of the Congo. Because we could not conceive of a Congolese government that would continue to be headed by a governor general, we realized that it was not true independence that was being promised us. . . . The whole population came to its feet, the whole population demanded immediate independence. And we have stated that we would mobilize all the men, all the women, all the children throughout this nation in the service of the Congolese revolution, in the service of peaceful revolution, because our doctrine, our basic doctrine, is based on nonviolence. On this point the population—thousands and thousands of persons—were seen to agree with us. No one was willing any longer to follow the administration. Every effort was made to stop me. The local administration mounted a gratuitous plot against me. An emissary from the Sûreté was sent here . . . And immediately afterward, there was a warrant put out for my arrest. . . . And then I was thrown in prison. I was brutally arrested, thrown into a pitch-black little cell, made to lie on the bare floor—and it was only when I protested and asked for a blanket that I was given one. A week later I was transferred to the military camp, where I spent a month in a shower-room lavatory that had no opening whatsoever. . . . Everything possible was done to break my spirit, but I knew that in every country in the world freedom is the ideal for which all men in all times have fought and died. Having made a choice, that of serving my country . . . I was jeered at, vilified, dragged in the mud—simply because I insisted on freedom for our country. I have never been against whites, I have never been against people, but what I have always rebelled against was injustice, and this regime that we have now gone beyond. . . . But for years now in the Congo we have had to bow our heads if we wanted the administration and certain colonial circles to treat us decently. We have always had to say *amen*, we have always had to say *yes* when we should have said *no*, but when a man wants to defend his country, when a man wants to defend the cause of freedom, a label is immediately pinned to him: he is a revolutionary, an agitator, a hoodlum—every possible label. They appeared on the scene immediately. I was handcuffed and knocked about. They carried me away; I was not even allowed to walk. From the prison to the truck, they tossed me about like a stick of wood; I was taken to the airfield, and immediately thrown into an airplane; they twisted my neck; I was badly mistreated. . . . I arrived in Elizabethville and came out of the airplane like a common bandit, whereupon several Europeans amused themselves by taking photographs of me.

Lumumba could well have repeated this statement word for word, exactly a year later in January, 1961, when he landed in Elizabethville, a prisoner of his most implacable adversaries, less than seven months after the independence of the Congo.

On June 30, 1960, at the ceremonies granting the Congo its independence, King Baudouin said:

People of the Congo, my country and I realize with joy and emotion that the Congo, in full accord and friendship with Belgium, has this thirtieth day of June, 1960, been granted independence and international sovereignty.

President Kasavubu followed him on the speakers' platform:

We cannot help but feel the weight of our responsibilities and ask God, in an attitude of profound humbleness, to protect our people and guide all its leaders.

But Patrice Lumumba, the Prime Minister of the first Congolese government, wanted above all to hail the struggle for independence, the victory that had been won, and the future that remained to be built:

We have known that the law was never the same for whites and blacks, for it made special concessions to the former, and was cruel and inhuman to the latter. We have been aware of the horrible suffering of those imprisoned for political opinions or religious beliefs; exiles in their own country, their lot was truly worse than death itself. . . . We who have known bodily suffering because cf colonialist oppression say to you: all that is now over and done with. The Congo has been proclaimed a Republic and our beloved country is now in the hands of its own children. We are about to begin another struggle together, my brothers, my sisters, a glorious struggle that will lead our country to peace, to prosperity, and to greatness. Together we will bring about social justice and assure that everyone receives equitable remuneration for his work. We will show the world what the black man can do when he works in freedom. [Applause.]

After the Belgian military intervention, during the
troubled month of July, 1960, Patrice Lumumba addressed
a crowd in Stanleyville, his faithful city:

We want the Congo to be a truly free country, a country whose inhabitants, black and white, will live in peace.
We must bring about human charity and fraternity in
our country. We must protect those Europeans who have
remained among us. We must prove that the Congolese
people are an honest people. There are no more tribes
in the Congo. There are no more Bakongos or Bangalas,
there are no more Wagenias; we have only one free people. We are all citizens and we must safeguard our national unity. Yesterday the Europeans sought to divide
us; they sought to divide the Bakongo and the Bangala;
they sought to divide Kasavubu and Lumumba; but we
shall prove to all these people that today we are united,
that we are going to safeguard our national unity, for it
is this unity that will make the Congo a great nation
in the heart of Africa, and tomorrow the Congo will
play a great role in the liberation of the remainder of
Africa. . . .
We wish today to turn the leadership of the army, the
administration, the police, and all supervisory posts over
to Congolese, and the Europeans who remain with us will
be mere advisers. And we want these leaders to assume
their posts conscientiously, competently, and patriotically.
We must part company with any Congolese, even if it be
Kasavubu or Lumumba, who will not work for the national cause. We want honest people, people who will
work for the country. We want people in a few months
to say: the Congo is truly a free country. And the man
who is named our Chief Commissioner or the Com-
mandant of the Force Publique, though he may not know
French, will speak in Swahili or in Lingala: we have our
national Flemish. [Laughter and applause; shouts of
Uhuru!]
    . . . And then, all of us together, dear brothers, dear
sisters, workers and employees, intellectuals and manual

laborers, rich and poor, Africans and Europeans, Catholics and Protestants, Kibanguists and Kitawalists, all of us together will build a great nation. Orientale Province must be a model province. There must not be the slightest trouble in Orientale Province. The peace of not a single European must be disturbed; not a single cry must ring out against a European, even those who treated us badly yesterday; they must be welcomed like brothers, we must give proof of our goodness. It is you who are going to be the honor of our Republic; it is you who are going to be the glory of our young country. We are going to overcome and go beyond every present obstacle. I have always said to you: we have no arms; we do not need arms. Let us mobilize to liberate our country. You listened to me. Today the country is liberated. *Uhuru* is here. [Shouts of *Uhuru;* applause.]

Today I give you yet another rallying cry: order must reign in Orientale Province, peace must reign. If anyone comes to you and says: "Let us attack so-and-so, let us attack a white," attack that black, because anyone who says that is from the PNP, and is the enemy of our freedom. . . . [Applause.]

Returning from a trip to the United States and around Africa, Lumumba came back to Leopoldville to find that a coalition had been formed among his adversaries, determined to cause his downfall by any possible means. Harried and threatened, Lumumba passionately denounced those who were attacking him:

We are being attacked because we will no longer bow down. We are being attacked because the members of the Congolese government are honest men who will have nothing to do with corruption. They have tried to buy us; they have tried to buy me for millions; I refused; I will not accept a cent for my people. And today the Belgian government has gotten money together to buy malcontents and die-hards throughout the country who day by day, in their newspapers, in their press, are mounting an organized campaign against the government, against the nation. Bishops have abandoned their mission of spreading the gospel to meddle in affairs of State. . . . We will not tolerate that. Our government is never going to meddle in the affairs of the Church. Freedom of religion will be guaranteed in our constitution. Catholics will pray in their churches, Protestants in theirs, Kibanguists in theirs, Kitawalists in theirs: everyone will pray in his own church and the State will protect all citizens and the government will respect all opinions, all religions. . . . [Applause.]

It has been said here in Leopoldville that a splinter group of Bakongo are going to proclaim their independence. This will never come to pass. The Chief of State himself, Mr. Kasavubu, President of the Abako, has sworn before the entire nation that he will watch over the unity of the country, that he will safeguard territorial integrity, and I know that Kasavubu does not agree with these Fascists. I know that Kasavubu is an upright man, an honest man, who sees the interests of the country, but I know also that there are a few who are discontented because they did not get ministerial portfolios in the central government and are working against Kasavubu and against the country. [Applause.]

Speaking before an African conference that met in Leopoldville at the end of August, 1960, Lumumba, embittered by the support lent the Katanga secession by certain outsiders, was eager to proclaim his faith in the unity of Africa. For him, Africa and the Congo had a common destiny, inextricably linked together as they were by the same ideals and facing the same perils:

Everyone has realized that if the Congo dies, all Africa will be plunged into the night of defeat and servitude. This is, once again, living proof of the unity of Africa. This is the concrete proof of this unity without which we could not exist in the face of the ravening appetites of imperialism. We are here to defend Africa, our patrimony, together. We must confront the concerted action of the imperialist powers, of whom the Belgian colonialists are only the instrument, with the united front of the free peoples and the peoples still struggling in Africa. We must confront the enemies of freedom with a coalition of free men. And our common lot is hanging in the balance here in the Congo at this moment. Here, indeed, a new act in the emancipation and the rehabilitation of Africa is being staged. Pursuing the struggle whose prime objective is to save the dignity of African man, the Congolese people have chosen immediate and total independence. In so doing, they knew that they would not rid themselves of the imprint of colonialism in one fell swoop, that juridical independence was only a first step, that the effort that must still be made would take time and perhaps be even harder. We have not chosen the easy path, but rather that of the pride and the freedom of man. [Applause.]

We have realized that so long as a country is not independent, so long as it has not assumed its destiny, it lacks what is most essential. And this remains true whatever the standard of living of those who have been colonized may be, whatever the positive aspects of a colonial system may be. We have imposed our will, which sought rapid independence with no intermediary period, with no compromises, all the more forcefully because we had been denied, depersonalized, demeaned. What, moreover, would it have availed us to wait, to negotiate further when we were well aware that sooner or later we would have to review everything, rethink everything by ourselves, create new structures suited to the needs of a truly African evolution, adapt for our own purposes the methods that had been forced upon us, and above all find ourselves once again, get rid of the mental attitudes, the complexes, the habits that colonization had instilled in us for centuries. The choice that was offered us was none other than this alternative: freedom or the prolongation of our enslavement. There can be no compromise between freedom and slavery. [Applause.]

The crucial hour was at hand. On September 5, 1960, at 8:10 A.M., came a sensational turn of events. During an English lesson broadcast by the Leopoldville radio, President Kasavubu came before the microphone:

My dear fellow citizens: I have an extremely important announcement to make to you. The Chief Burgomaster[1] named by the King of Belgium, as provided by the basic provisional Law, has betrayed the office conferred upon him. He has had recourse to arbitrary measures that have provoked discord within the government and among the people. He has governed arbitrarily. He has deprived numerous citizens of their fundamental liberties and even now is in the process of plunging the country into a fearful civil war. That is why I have deemed it necessary to dismiss the government.

Patrice Lumumba immediately took to the air to deliver a passionate answer in the language of the African masses:

I wish to announce that a Council of Ministers will be held this evening to examine the situation that has just been created this evening by the unexpected declaration of Mr. Joseph Kasavubu, who has publicly betrayed the nation. I was not consulted by Mr. Kasavubu, nor has any minister or any member of parliament been consulted. Democracy requires that a government rule only if it is elected by the people and has the confidence of the people. We enjoy such confidence. We have proved to the people, to the entire world, that the national popular government which you freely elected to defend your

[1] President Kasavubu was referring, of course, to Prime Minister Patrice Lumumba.—*Editor's note.*

interests, to defend your national patrimony, has worked up to the present in the superior interest of the nation.

At this point Lumumba declared:

In the name of the democratically elected government, in the name of all our elected officers, all those who voted for Kasavubu, I proclaim that we withdraw our vote. The popular government remains at its post. Beginning today, I proclaim that Kasavubu, who has betrayed the nation, who has betrayed the people, is no longer Chief of State because he has collaborated with the Belgians and the Flemish. [Applause. Cries of "Long live Lumumba!" "Down with Kasavubu!" "Down with saboteurs!"]

The show of force was to have an outcome favorable to Lumumba's adversaries, in particular after the coup d'état of Colonel Mobutu and the failure of Lumumba's attempt to reach Stanleyville at the end of November, 1960.

In January, 1961, in prison at the military camp of Thysville, Lumumba managed to get through a final message, which was recorded by "Italia Canta":

In our good fortune as in bad, I will always remain at your side. It is with you that I have fought to liberate this country from foreign domination. It is with you that I am fighting to consolidate our national independence. It is with you that I will fight to safeguard the integrity and the national unity of the Republic of the Congo.

We have made a choice, that of serving our country loyally and faithfully. We shall never depart from this path. Freedom is the ideal for which, in all times down through the centuries, men have fought and died. The Congo could not escape this reality and it is thanks to our heroic and glorious struggle that we have valiantly won our independence and our dignity as free men.

A letter from Patrice Lumumba managed to reach his wife Pauline:

My beloved companion:

I write you these words without knowing whether they will ever reach you, or when they will reach you, and whether I will still be alive when you read them. All through my struggle for the independence of my country, I have never doubted for a single instant that in the end the sacred cause to which my comrades and I have devoted our whole lives would triumph. But what we wanted for our country—its right to an honorable life, to a dignity without a blemish, to an independence without restrictions—Belgian colonialism and its Western allies, who found direct and indirect, deliberate and non-deliberate support among certain high officials of the United Nations (that body in which we placed all our trust when we called upon it for assistance), have never wanted.

They have corrupted certain of our compatriots, they have bought others, they have done their part in twisting the truth and sullying our independence. What else can I say? That whether I am dead, alive, free, or in prison by order of the colonialists, it is not my person that counts. It is the Congo, it is our poor people whose independence has been turned into a cage in which we are looked at from outside the bars, sometimes with charitable compassion, sometimes with joy and delight. . . .

We are not alone. Africa, Asia, and the free and freed peoples in every corner of the earth will always be found at the side of the millions of Congolese who will not abandon the struggle until the day when there will be no more colonizers and no more of their mercenaries in our country. To my children whom I leave behind and whom I may perhaps not see again, I want people to say that the future of the Congo is beautiful and that it expects them, as it expects every Congolese, to fulfill the sacred task of reconstructing our independence and our sovereignty; for without justice there is no dignity, and without independence there are no free men. . . .

History will have its say some day, but it will not be the history that is taught in the United Nations, in

Washington, Paris, or Brussels, but the one that is taught in the countries that have freed themselves of colonialism and its puppets. Africa will write its own history, and both north and south of the Sahara it will be a history full of glory and dignity.

Do not weep for me, my companion—I know that my country, now suffering so much, will be able to defend its independence and its freedom.

Long live the Congo! Long live Africa!

PATRICE

B

Telegram from Justin Bomboko to the UN Commission of Inquiry on the Congo

c/o His Honor the Secretary General of the UN
New York, N.Y., January 21, 1961

We have learned of the meeting of the UN Commission of Inquiry to examine the Lumumba, Okito, Mpolo situation. We would like to communicate the following to the six members of the Commission:

a) Mr. Lumumba and his friends are and remain in the Congo. Their transfer from Thysville to Elizabethville was not carried out with evil intentions.

b) The rumors that they have been molested proved untrue. They are quite well and much better than the prisoners in Stanleyville, whose inhuman treatment seems not to concern the Afro-Asian bloc, an attitude which surprises all Congolese citizens.

c) In his press conference, held in Leopoldville after the transfer of Lumumba and his co-prisoners, Mr. Wachuku, President of the Commission, was objective; nonetheless he recognized the unwarranted interference in interior Congolese affairs and expressed regrets about this intereference.

d) Commission's good offices now making trip across the Congo to find a solution to the Congolese crisis;

we find that the meeting of the Commission of Inquiry might influence this commission which is working on the scene and which should remain neutral. We insist on non-interference in Congolese affairs.

> (*signed*) Bomboko, President of the Board of Commissioners General and Commissioner General for Foreign Affairs

c

Message from the President of Katanga (Moise Tshombe) to Dag Hammarskjöld, February 1, 1961

The transfer of Mr. Lumumba to Katanga is due to the initiative and the request of His Honor, the President of the Congo, His Excellency Mr. Joseph Kasavubu, and I am quite surprised at the interest manifested by the UN as regards the ex-Prime Minister, who, in fact, has been recognized as guilty of genocide by the international organization.

Furthermore, in view of the number of crimes committed by Lumumba against the nation and the Congolese peoples, it is essential that the authorities of the ex-Belgian Congo remain the only judges, without foreign intervention, of the treatment and fate reserved for him. This procedure is accepted in regard to other countries where analogous situations are being resolved. . . .

Because of the unfortunate reactions which have always followed Mr. Lumumba's inflammatory words, I believe that there is reason, in order to calm everyone's mood, to avoid all contact by Mr. Lumumba with the outside world.

D

Declaration by Godefroid Munongo to the Press, February 13, 1961

I would be lying if I said that the death of Lumumba makes me sad. You know my feelings on the subject: he is a common criminal who is responsible for the death in Katanga of thousands of people and for tens of thousands in Kasai, without counting the persecutions and deaths in Orientale Province and Kivu. . . .

I am certain what the result of a trial of Lumumba would have been: he would have been condemned to death. This does not mean that I would not have preferred that Lumumba and his accomplices be judged.

It was in any case their fault; they should not have escaped into a pro-governmental region at a time when their own friends in the UN were stirring up the Katangese population to such a point of excitement.

I, of course, know that the UN will say that this is a political machination and that we ourselves assassinated them. Such an accusation is inevitable. Even if Lumumba had died from illness, old age, or a natural death in Katanga, we would still have been accused of assassinating him simply because his death took place in Katanga.

I am going to speak to you frankly and toughly, as is my habit. We have been accused of assassination; I answer: prove it. . . .

E

Note (No. 10-442) from Moise Tshombe to a UN Representative, February 15, 1961

The President of the State of Katanga regrets that he will not be able to see General Yassu now but, knowing the reason for his visit, he wants it known that the government of Katanga is opposed to the visit of an international Commission of Inquiry simply because this would be a threat to the sovereignty of the populations of the ex-Belgian Congo, and no country has yet accepted such an investigation.

The Katangese authorities do, in any case, carry on investigations into such matters regularly. Furthermore we refer you to the official communiqué which will be given to the press today, a copy of which is attached herewith.

F

Exchange of Letters between Mr. Dayal, Special Representative of the UN in the Congo, and Mr. Tshombe

Letter from Dayal to Tshombe, February 15, 1961

The destitute families of Messrs. Lumumba, Mpolo, and Okito visited me today STOP They asked me to use the good offices of the UN to see that the remains of the deceased be returned to them STOP It is, in my opinion, imperative that we accede to such a demand for humanitarian reasons and I have the honor of being the intermediary for these victims of a cruel tragedy by asking you to carry out this request immediately STOP In all civilized countries, those who are in mourning can count on the authorities to help them to give the deceased the homage that is their due STOP In the Congo, in particular, I think that Bantu traditions join with Christian traditions and make it a sacred obligation for the parents to weep and to bury their dead in the presence of the family and in their native land STOP I am thus persuaded that you should take the necessary measures which would allow the families of Lumumba, Okito, and Mpolo to acquit themselves of this obligation STOP These fami-

lies have also asked me to aid them to return to their
native lands in order to mourn and to prepare the funeral
STOP   I will attend to their desires immediately STOP   If
the absence of a means of transportation is an obstacle to
the transfer of the mortal remains, this could be carried
out by UN planes leaving from Elizabethville.

Letter from Tshombe to Dayal, February 18, 1961

The government of Katanga has perfectly understood
the humanitarian aspect of the request by the interested
families but regrets that it will not be able to respond
favorably to the request at this time under present circumstances. In fact, a transfer of the mortal remains
would result, no matter what the precautions, in a divul-
gence of the name of the village that we have wanted to
remain anonymous and a renewal of the passions that
everyone wishes to see stilled.

The question might eventually be re-examined when
the situation is entirely calm once again.

Letter from Tshombe to Dayal, February 22, 1961

The President of the State of Katanga, while understanding the humanitarian aspects of the question, would
like to bring to the attention of Mr. Dayal the fact that
the Bantu customs he speaks of are entirely opposed to
all exhumation, even if carried out by the family in the
case of a natural death. According to Bantu tradition, it
is formally forbidden to unearth, even though only for
several seconds, a body which is covered by earth, because the deceased might be gravely injured and his soul
might haunt those who survive him. When a member of
the family has not been able to attend the funeral cere-

mony, the Bantu custom simply permits him to participate *a posteriori* in the funeral ceremony which takes place on the tomb and is of a religious character. Obviously, such a ceremony would reveal the name of the village where the fugitives were buried. Incidentally, this ignorance of Bantu customs once more demonstrates the total inability of the UN to impose its authority in territories it is ignorant of. Furthermore, the President of the State of Katanga does not agree with Mr. Dayal's statements that the sadness caused throughout the world by the news of the assassination of the prisoners committed in Katanga will not be appeased until light is shed on the case and justice is rendered. The emotion in question is only hypocritical and artificial, having been stirred up by countries which have committed innumerable assassinations and it will die down by itself if it is not artificially fed. The President of the State of Katanga vehemently protests the word "assassination" used by Mr. Dayal. . . .

G

Resolution of the Security Council

The Security Council

Having examined the situation in the Congo,

Having learned with profound regret of the death of the Congolese leaders Mr. Patrice Lumumba, Mr. Maurice Mpolo, and Mr. Joseph Okito,

Profoundly concerned about the grave repercussions of these crimes and about the risk of a civil war and the general spilling of blood in the Congo, as well as by the threat to international peace and security,

Noting the report of the Special Representative of the Secretary General (S/4691), dated February 12, 1961, which reveals that there is a grave possibility of civil war and discusses the preparations being made toward this end . . .

Decides that an impartial inquiry will take place immediately with the hope of discovering the circumstances of the death of Mr. Lumumba and of his colleagues and of prosecuting the parties responsible for these crimes. . . .

(UN document S/4976; resolution of February 21, 1961)

Chronology

The Independent Congo, 1960–61

Principal stages before Lumumba's death:
    1960

June 23	The first Congolese government, presided over by Patrice Lumumba, installed by the Chamber (74 votes out of 137)
June 24	Joseph Kasavubu elected chief of state by the combined Chambers (150 votes against 43 and 11 abstentions)
June 30	Declaration of Independence of the Republic of the Congo
July 5	Troubles at the heart of the Force Publique
July 9	Belgian military intervention in Elizabethville
July 11	Declaration of the secession of Katanga

July 14	The UN Security Council decides to intervene and relations between the Congo and Belgium are broken off
August 8	Creation of the mining state of South Kasai
August 13	Lumumba demands withdrawal of white troops of the UN
August 31	Withdrawal of last metropolitan Belgian troops and conclusion of the Pan-African Conference in Leopoldville
September 5	Rupture between Kasavubu and Lumumba; Kasavubu announces the creation of a government headed by Joseph Ileo; bloody battles and repressions by the ANC against the Baluba of Kasai
September 14	Colonel Mobutu neutralizes political institutions and their heads
September 19	Institution of a Board of Commissioners General and failure of the first attempts at reconciliation between Kasavubu and Lumumba
October 10	Lumumba is put in a guarded residence under the supervision of the ANC and the protection of the UN
November 15	Antoine Gizenga and General Lundula take control of Stanleyville

November 21–22	Bloody incidents at the Ghana Embassy in Leopoldville between the ANC and the UN; Colonel Nkokolo killed
November 27	Lumumba leaves his residence in Leopoldville and tries to reach Stanleyville
November 28	First encounter between Kasavubu and Tshombe in Brazzaville
December 1	Lumumba arrested by the ANC–Mobutu soldiers; Gilbert Pongo confirms transfer of Lumumba to Leopoldville the next day
December 3	Lumumba transferred to Camp Hardy in Thysville, in the Bas-Congo
December 15	Meeting of the so-called "moderate" Congolese leaders and plans for a national Round Table Conference on the structures of the state
December 25	Gizengist authorities in Stanleyville secure control of Bukavu

1961

January 1	Failure of attempt to retake Bukavu by Colonel Mobutu's troops
January 9	The ANC–Lundula takes control of North Katanga; a Lualaba, anti-Tshombist government installed

January 13	Tensions, discontent, and mutiny among the ANC soldiers at Camp Hardy in Thysville
January 14	Soldiers begin to agitate at Camp Nkokolo in Leopoldville
January 17	Transfer of Lumumba, Mpolo, and Okito to Elizabethville and assassination of the three prisoners

January 17, 1961

In the Congo

In Leopoldville:

Joseph Kasavubu is chief of state
Joseph Mobutu is head of the army
Justin Bomboko presides over the Board of Commissioners General
Victor Nendaka directs the Sûreté

In Stanleyville:

Antoine Gizenga is head of the Lumumbist government
Victor Lundula is head of the army

In Elizabethville:

Moise Tshombe is chief of the secessionist state of Katanga

Godefroid Munongo is the Minister of the Interior

In North Katanga:

Prosper Mwamba Ilunga heads a government hostile to Tshombe

In Africa

In Brazzaville:

Fulbert Youlou organizes a referendum

In Guinea:

Sekou Touré is re-elected chief of state

In Rhodesia:

Roy Welensky supports the Katangese secession

In the United Arab Republic:

Pierre Mulele represents the Stanleyville authorities in talks with Nasser

In Rwanda:

The deposition of King Kigeri and the proclamation of a republic are imminent

In Ethiopia:

The repression is harsh after the failure of the revolution of 1960

In the World

In Brazil:

> Janio Quadros will soon be reinvested as the president of the republic

In Paris:

> General de Gaulle prepares to negotiate with the G.P.R.A. (Gouvernement Provisional de la République Algérienne—Provisional Government of the Algerian Republic) about Algeria.

In Washington, D.C.:

> Kennedy prepares to take on the duties of President

In Cuba:

> Diplomatic relations between Havana and Washington are broken off.

In Power Are:

> In Russia: Nikita Khrushchev
> In India: Jawalaharl Nehru
> In China: Mao Tse-tung
> In Great Britain: Harold Macmillan
> In Belgium: Gaston Eyskens
> In Ghana: Kwame Nkrumah
> In the United States: John F. Kennedy

Biographical Notes

Adoula, Cyrille Co-founder of the MNC and secretary of the FGTK in Leopoldville from 1959–60; member of the provisional government of Joseph Ileo in February, 1961; head of the government from August, 1961, to July, 1964; in exile from November, 1964, to October, 1965; ambassador to Brussels, then to Washington, after General Mobutu took power; Minister of Foreign Affairs since August, 1969.

Akunda, Louis Head of Mpolo's cabinet in June, 1960, as Secretary of Youth and Sports; Minister of Youth of the Gizenga government in Stanleyville in 1961; in 1962, head of the cabinet as Minister of Justice in Sankuru, then Minister of Public Works in December, 1963; in May, 1964, Minister of Employment and State Insurance in Sankuru. Imprisoned in Leopoldville in 1965. There has been no news of him since 1966.

Bintou, Raphael Secretary General of the FGTK Union of Katanga, Kivu, Kasai in 1960; Provincial Counselor in Katanga, then in South Kasai; headed the social commission of Conaco, Tshombe's party, in 1965; President of FGTK in 1966; Administrator of the Gecomin since January, 1967; Assistant Secretary General of the UNTC in 1967; Vice-Minister of Labor from March to August, 1969.

Bobozo, Louis   Commander of Camp Hardy in Thysville in 1960–61; Commander of the 4th Group of the Congolese National Army (ANC) in Elizabethville in March, 1963; Major General in June, 1964; commander in chief of the ANC in November, 1965.

Bocheley-Davidson, Egide   Elected to the Chamber in the MNC–Lumumba party; spokesman for the Lumumbist opposition to Cyrille Adoula in 1962–63; arrested in Leopoldville on September 29, 1963; rejoined the National Council of Liberation (CNL) in Brazzaville; member of the Supreme Council of the Revolution (CSR) since April, 1965.

Bolamba, Antoine-Roger   Secretary of State for Information in the Lumumba government in 1960; Assistant Secretary General of the MNC (provisional central committee), June, 1962; Minister of Information of the Adoula government from April, 1963, to July 10, 1964; deputy *locum tenens* on the Conaco list in May, 1965 (Cuvette-Centrale); in February, 1966, named head of press services for the president of the republic, and chief of the administrative service of the office of the President since May, 1969.

Bolikango, Jean   President of PUNA, unsuccessful candidate for the presidency of the republic in June, 1960; Vice-Prime Minister of the Adoula government in August, 1961; national PUNA deputy in 1965; Minister of Public Works in the Mulamba government but removed by President Mobutu in April, 1966; Member of the MPR since July, 1968.

Bomboko, Justin   Ex-student of the Université Libre in Brussels; elected to the Chamber from the Union

Mongo; Minister of Foreign Affairs in the first Congolese government; President of the Board of Commissioners General in September, 1960; minister in the Ileo and Adoula governments from 1961–64; national deputy for Unicentrale in 1965 and head of Foreign Affairs in the Mulamba government in November, 1965, and in the governments following until August, 1969; ambassador to Washington since August, 1969.

Cardoso, Mario-Philippe President-spokesman for MNC–Lumumba at the Belgo-Congolese economic conference in May, 1960; assistant at Lovanium in 1959–60; Commissioner General of National Education in September, 1960; charge d'affaires, then minister, then ambassador of the Congo in Washington from 1962–65; ambassador to London in 1966; ambassador to Rabat from October to March, 1969; Minister of Education since March, 1969.

Delvaux, Albert President of, and elected to, the Chamber from the Luka party in Kwango in 1960; resident minister in Belgium from the first Congolese government, then in the provisional government of Ileo; Minister of Public Works from July, 1962, to July, 1964; elected to the Chamber from the Luka party in 1965; Member of the MPR since July, 1968.

Diaka, Bernardin Member, then chief, of Patrice Lumumba's cabinet in 1960; Gizenga's ambassador to Peking in April, 1961; expelled from China in September, 1961; Provincial Minister from Kwilu in 1962 and 1963; National Deputy of the Parti Solidaire Africain (PSA, African Solidarity Party) in 1965 and Minister of Middle Classes in the Mulamba government; ambassador to

Brussels in 1966–1967; first national secretary of the MPR from April to October, 1967; Minister of Education; resigned as Minister and member of the political bureau in July, 1968.

Gbenye, Christophe   Minister of the Interior in the first Congolese government in June, 1960, and in the Lumumbist government in Stanleyville in November, 1960; occupied the same functions in the Adoula government of reconciliation in August, 1961; president of the MNC–Lumumba in 1963; went to Brazzaville in October, 1963, and presided over the National Committee of Liberation (CNL), the political organ of the rebellion; on September 5, 1964, he was in Stanleyville as president of the République Populaire du Congo (Popular Republic of the Congo), which he was forced to leave at the time of the Belgo-American operation in November, 1964; has lived in Kampala since 1966.

Gizenga, Antoine   President of the Parti Solidaire Africain (PSA) and elected to the Chamber by this party in May, 1960; Vice-Prime Minister in the Lumumba government in June, 1960, he assumed control of the Lumumbist government in Stanleyville from November, 1960, to August, 1961, at which time he was promoted to Vice-Prime Minister in Adoula's government of reconciliation. Dismissed by a vote of the Chamber on January 16, 1962, he was transferred and detained on the island of Bula Mbemba until July, 1964. Founder of the Parti Lumumbist Unifié, he was placed under house arrest by Tshombe on October 1, 1964, and then liberated by General Mobutu in the end of 1965. He has been out of the country since 1966.

Grenfell, Georges   National deputy of the MNC–Lumumba; Minister of State in June, 1960; arrested and jailed in December, 1960; member of the Gizenga government in Stanleyville in March, 1961; president of the province of Haut-Congo in 1961; imprisoned in Makala in 1964; liberated, in Leopoldville since 1966.

Ileo, Joseph   Author of the manifesto "Conscience Africaine" in 1956; co-founder of the MNC; president of the central provisional government of February, 1961, and minister in Adoula's government of national reconciliation; in 1963, resident minister in Katanga; in 1964, president of the Constitutional Commission of Luluabourg. Administrator of the Imprimerie Concordia (Concordia Book Company) and member of the Council of Lovanium Université. Senator in 1965; President of the ONRD since August, 1967 and member of the political bureau of the MPR since March, 1969.

Kalonji, Albert   President of the so-called Kalonji wing of the MNC in November 1959; National Deputy in June, 1960; President-Mulopwe of South Kasai in 1960–61; dismissed from his parliamentary functions at the end of 1961 and condemned; in exile from January, 1963 (notably in Spain); Minister of Agriculture in the Tshombe government in July, 1964, and Senator Conaco in 1965; he retired from political life in December, 1966.

Kamitatu, Cléophas   Provincial President of the PSA, president of the province of Leopoldville in June, 1960; minister in the Adoula government from 1962–64; elected National Deputy for the PSA in 1965; headed the anti-

Tshombe front with Nendaka (FDC); was Minister of Foreign Affairs in the Kimba government in October, 1965. He was also administrator of Sabena. Implicated in the so-called "Pentacost" trial, he was condemned in 1966 to five years in prison; freed on November 23, 1967.

Kandolo, Damien   Head of Lumumba's cabinet in June, 1960; Assistant Commissioner General for the Interior in September, 1960; attaché to the cabinet of Adoula, then Secretary General of the Interior; dismissed in 1964; in Belgium until the eviction of Tshombe; administrator to the Colectric (Cominière group); president of the Société des Transports en commun du Congo (Congolese Transportation Company); President of the Gecomin since September, 1968.

Kanza, Daniel   Vice-President of the Abako but expelled from this party in February, 1960; first mayor of Leopoldville from October, 1960, to June, 1962; President of the Alliance des Congolais (Alliance of the Congolese); in November, 1965, announced his intention of running for the presidency of the republic.

Kanza, Thomas   First Congolese to receive a diploma from a university; son of Daniel Kanza (see above); Minister-Delegate to the UN in the government of June, 1960. Having resigned his post as ambassador of the Congo to London under the second Adoula government, he was, beginning in September, 1964, the foreign representative of the République Populaire du Congo (RPC, Popular Republic of the Congo) and of Gbenye. Left this post in 1966; has lived in London since then.

Kasavubu, Joseph   President of the Abako; national deputy, then president of the republic from June, 1960, to November, 1965; senator in 1966. Died March 24, 1969.

Kashamura, Anicet   Director of the Centre de Régroupement Africain (Céréa, Center of African Regroupment) in Bukavu; Minister of Information in June, 1960; took power in Kivu in the name of the Lumumbist authorities of Stanleyville at the beginning of 1961; minister under Gizenga in May, 1961, then, after various political misfortunes, lived in exile in Africa and in Europe.

Kasongo, Joseph-Georges   National deputy of the MNC–Lumumba in the district of Haut-Congo; president of the Chamber of Representatives; not re-elected in March, 1962; played an important role in the attempts at reconciliation between Lumumba and Kasavubu in September, 1960; Vice-Prime Minister in the Adoula government in April, 1963; elected Senator from Maniema in January, 1966.

Kazadi, Ferdinand   Ex-student at Lovanium; Commissioner General for Defense in September, 1960; in charge of the transfer of Lumumba to Elizabethville on January 17, 1961; Provincial Minister of South Kasai in June, 1961; elected National Deputy from Panaco in 1965; Minister of Public Works in the Mobutu government since August, 1969.

Kibwe, Jean-Baptiste   Provincial Deputy of Conakat in 1960; Minister of Finance of Katanga until the end of the secession; Minister of East Katanga in 1963; Vice-President of the Conakat; minister of South Katanga in 1966; President of the Gecomin in January, 1967; arrested in February, 1968; condemned on March 13, 1969 by the Court of Appeals to fifteen months in prison and a fine.

Kimba, Evariste   Senator from Katanga in 1960; Minister of Foreign Affairs in the Tshombe government during the secession; Provincial Minister of East Katanga in 1963; Secretary General and elected National Deputy of the Entente Balubakat in 1965; Prime Minister of the central government from October 13 to November 14, 1965; condemned to death and hanged at Kinshasa under indictment for participation in the so-called "Pentacost" plot in 1966.

Kiwele, Joseph   Provincial Deputy of Conakat, in May, 1960; Minister of Education of Katanga; President of the Council of the University of Elizabethville during the secession; died on November 15, 1961.

Lassiry, Gabriel   Lumumbist militant; appointed chargé de mission by Gizenga in 1961; Provincial Minister of Maniema in September, 1962; National Deputy of the MNC–Lumumba in 1965.

Lubuma, Valentin   Head of the Gizenga cabinet in Stanleyville in 1960–61; in January, 1962, imprisoned in Stanleyville; director of the political bureau of the PSA in June, 1963; in June, 1964, director of the political bureau of the central provisional committee of the PSA–Gizenga; member of the Gizenga cabinet after July, 1964; in Leopoldville in 1966.

Lumumba, Patrice Born on July 2, 1925, in Onalua, territory of Katako-Kombe (Sankuru-Kasai), of the Otetela tribe. Went through secondary school. In 1954, postal clerk in Stanleyville. In 1957, he was employed by an important brewery in Leopoldville and soon became its commercial director. He left this company in October, 1959, to devote himself entirely to the direction of the MNC.

In 1955, he was a militant in the ranks of the Cercle Libéral.[1] In 1956, Provincial President of the Association du Personnel Indigène de la Colonie (Association of Indigenous Workers of the Colony) for Orientale Province, he traveled to Belgium to study. From October, 1958, onward, he was one of the most active promoters of the MNC. In December, 1958, he participated in the Pan-African Conference at Accra, the source of his idea of active neutralism. In the Luluabourg Congress of April, 1959, he outlined the objectives of a national and supra-tribal party.

On November 1, 1959, he was arrested after the Stanleyville Congress. Liberated through intervention of the Minister of the Congo and all the Congolese leaders, he attended the Round Table Conference of the Belgians and Congolese in January–February, 1960. Named member of the Collège Executif Général (General Executive College) in March, 1960, he protested against the shipping of

[1] The Cercle Libéral was a Congolese offshoot of the intellectual Parti Libéral de Belgique, a party that, since the nineteenth century, was opposed to the Belgian Catholics on the question of schools in particular. The fact that Lumumba was a member is explained by the fact that he was sponsored by the liberal Minister of Colonies at that time, Auguste Buisseret, promoter of the official educational policy of the Congo, which meant that he favored the development of an educational policy which differed from the policy of the missionary churches.

reinforcements of Belgian troops to the Congo in May, 1960. Elected National Deputy with a majority of 84,602 votes in the Stanleyville district.

On June 23, the Chambers invested the group he headed with ministerial powers. Lumumba was both Prime Minister and Minister of Defense in this government.

On September 5, President Kasavubu dismissed him, but Lumumba got the Chamber to affirm the legitimacy of his government. As he attempted to reach Stanleyville, he was arrested and imprisoned in Thysville on December 2, 1960. Transferred to Katanga on January 17, 1961, he was killed soon after his arrival.

Lundula, Victor   Named General Commander in Chief of the National Congolese Army (ANC) in July, 1960; dismissed from his functions by President Kasavubu in September, 1960; commander of the Stanleyville group favorable to Gizenga at the end of 1960–61; adviser to the Defense Department from 1962–64; Senator from Sankuru in 1965; chancellor of National Tribes since 1966.

Mahamba, Alexander   Senator from Kivu; Minister of Property in June, 1960, then in August, 1961; Minister of Health in 1963; Secretary General of the Association of Lawyers at the end of 1964; condemned to death and hanged in Kinshasa, charged with having participated in the so-called "Pentacost" plot, 1966.

Massena, Joachim   Elected National Deputy from the PSA; Labor Minister in June, 1960, then in the Lumumbist government in Stanleyville in 1961; imprisoned in Leopoldville in 1963; liberated in July, 1964; kidnapped and assassinated in Binza the following September 7.

Matuba, Joseph   Assistant Administrative Director of the Sûreté; arrested and charged with forgery; living in Congo-Central since 1966.

Mbeka, Joseph   M.A. in Economics from Lovanium University; member of the cabinet as head of Economic Planning in July, 1960; Commissioner General for Economic Planning in September, 1960; representative from the Congo in the European Economic Committee (Common Market) from 1961 to October, 1965. Head of the cabinet of President Mobutu; ambassador to Paris in 1966; Vice-Minister of Finance since March, 1969.

Mbuyi, Joseph   Minister of Middle Classes in the first Congolese government; said to have been killed in Kasai at the end of 1960.

Moanda, Vital   Vice-President of the Abako in 1960; National Deputy in May, 1960; President of Kongo Central since its creation; governor of Orientale Province on January 3, 1967; arrested in July, 1967 and freed on August 29, 1968.

Mobutu, Joseph-Désiré   Ex-journalist; delegate from the MNC–Lumumba to Brussels in 1960; Secretary of State for the president of the Council in June, 1960; named Colonel Chief of Staff of the ANC in July, 1960. General since 1961 and commander in chief of the reunified ANC; Lieutenant General in 1965; president of the republic in November, 1965; also Minister of Veterans and Defense.

Mpolo, Maurice   Born in Inongo on March 4, 1928. Held different positions in private enterprises, in the administration, and the police; President of the MNC–Lumumba in Leopoldville; participated in the Round Table Conference in Brussels in January, 1960. Elected Provincial and National Deputy in the district of Lac Leopold II. Later resigned from his position of Provincial Deputy. Minister of Youth and Sports in the Lumumba government; named Colonel in the Congolese Army; dismissed on September 12, 1960, by Kasavubu, but named chief of the general staff by Lumumba; arrested at Mushie, then jailed in Thysville with Patrice Lumumba on December 12, 1960; transferred with him to Katanga on January 17, 1961, and killed there.

Mukamba, Jonas   Ex-student of the Catholic University of Louvain; Assistant Commissioner of Labor, then of Interior, in 1960; in charge of the transfer of Lumumba to Elizabethville on January 17, 1961; Provincial Minister of South Kasai from June, 1961, to May, 1965; National Deputy from Déco in 1965; Governor of South Kasai since June, 1965, and of East Kasai in April, 1966; governor of Equateur Province from December, 1966, to August, 1968; governor of Orientale Province in 1968; position revoked in October, 1968 under charge of fomenting tribal disturbances.

Mukenge, Barthélémy   President of the provincial government of Kasai from June, 1960, to June, 1962; President of the state of North Kasai; Minister in the Luluabourg government in September, 1962; created the Parti Social Démocrate Africain (PSDA, African Democratic Social Party) at Lulaubourg in 1963 and became its President General in 1965; deputy from the PSDA–Radeco in 1965; governor of Kivu Province since August, 1969.

Mulele, Pierre National Deputy of the PSA; Minister of National Education in June, 1960; member of the Gizenga government of Stanleyville in November, 1960, and its representative in Cairo; he traveled in Communist China, then from July, 1963, onward he organized and directed the guerrillas in Kwilu; executed at Kinshasa about October 8, 1968.

Munongo, Godefroid First president of the Conakat in 1958; Provincial Deputy, then Minister of the Interior, in Katanga from June, 1960, to the end of the secession; provincial Minister of East Katanga in 1963 and Minister of the Interior in the central government of Tshombe in 1964–65; governor of East Katanga in June, 1965, of South Katanga in April, 1966; suspended in November, 1966; removed from office December 25, 1966; arrested December 26, 1966 and freed August 29, 1968. Under house arrest in Kinshasa since then.

Mwamba, Rémy Co-founder and Secretary General of the Balubakat; Minister of Justice in the Lumumba government and then in the Gizenga government in Stanleyville; from August, 1961, to 1962, Minister of Justice of the Adoula government; President of the Common Katangese Front in Leopoldville in April, 1963; elected counselor of the PPC–Balubakat in January, 1964; imprisoned in Leopoldville in November, 1964; liberated on August 23, 1965.

Mwamba Ilunga, Prosper   National Deputy from the Balubakat in 1960; anti-secessionist spokesman in the Katangese Assembly, then forbidden to travel; president of the government of the Province of Lualaba in October–November, 1960; Provincial President of North Katanga in 1962–63, then president of the assembly of this province in 1963–64; imprisoned on orders of the Sûreté from May to August, 1964, and liberated in August, 1965; appointed to replace Bertin Mwamba on April 27, 1967.

Mwenda-Munongo, Antoine   Chief of the Bayeke; Provincial Counselor in Katanga and administrator of the Union Minière from May, 1965 to 1967.

Ndele, Albert   Masters degree in economics from the University of Lovanium; head of the cabinet for Finance in June, 1960; Vice-President of the Board of Commissioners General in September, 1960; governor of the Banque Nationale du Congo (National Bank of the Congo) in February, 1961, and Vice-President of the Council of the University of Lovanium.

Ndjoku, Colonel   Commander of the ANC in Luluabourg and collaborator of Mobutu; in 1962, chief of the Kasai garrison; retired from the ANC.

Nendaka, Victor   Vice-President of the MNC–Lumumba in 1959 and until April, 1960; head of the Sûreté of the interior from September–October 1960 to 1965: Minister of the Interior in the Tshombe government; elected deputy on the Conaco list in 1965; founded the anti-Tshombe front (FDC) in October, 1965; Minister of the Interior in the Kimba government, and Minister of

Communications and Transportation in the Mulamba government, then in the Mobutu government from 1966 to 1968; Minister of Finance from August, 1968 to August, 1969; ambassador to Bonn since August, 1969.

Ngalula, Joseph   Co-founder of the MNC; Prime Minister and Vice President of South Kasai in 1960–61; Minister of National Education in Adoula's government of reconciliation; President of South Kasai, then national deputy from Rapelu in 1965; president of the administrative council of the KDL–BCK since January, 1968.

Ngoma, Oscar   Commissioner of the Boma district in 1960; Administrative Director of the Sûreté from 1962–1965; commissioner of Bandundu Province in 1968; then of Equateur Province since August, 1969.

Nussbaumer, José   Commissioner General of the Interior in September, 1960; student at Louvain; Director of the European Bureau of the Agence Congolaise de Presse (Congolese Press Agency) from 1962–63, then press attaché at the Congolese Embassy in Brussels. Held no public office since 1966.

Nzuzi, Emmanuel   Secretary General of Youth for the MNC–Lumumba; organizer of the MNC militia; arrested after the assassination attempt against Commissioner Ndele; transferred to Bakwanga in the beginning of 1961 and executed there in February.

Okito, Joseph   Born in Lusambo (Kasai) on February 5, 1910. President and founder of the Union Rurale du Congo (URUCCO, the Rural Union of the Congo) at

the beginning of 1959. In 1960, he became president of
the MNC in Sankuru; participated in the Congrès d'Union
(Congress of Union) of the Akutshu-Anamongo of Lodja
in March, 1960; named senator of Kasai, and elected
vice-president of the Senate in June, 1960, then president
in September, 1960; arrested on November 20, 1960, at
Kikwit; jailed in Thysville on December 2, then transferred with Patrice Lumumba to Elizabethville on January 17, 1961, where he was killed.

Pinzi, Arthur   Mayor of Kalamu in 1958; National
Deputy from the Abako in 1960; Provincial Minister of
Kongo-Central in 1961, then Minister of Finance of the
central government from August, 1961, to April, 1962;
chargé d'affaires in the Ivory Coast in 1965; in Madrid
in 1966; relieved of his duties on October 4, 1967.

Pongo, Gilbert   Inspector of the Sûreté in September, 1960; in charge of the pursuit and capture of Patrice
Lumumba at the end of November, 1960; commander of
the ANC operation against Bukavu on January 1, 1961;
prisoner of the Gizengist authorities and executed in
Stanleyville in February, 1961.

Rudahindwa, Edmond   Elected National Deputy on
the Reco list in May, 1960, and in 1965; Minister of
Mines in the first Congolese government; member of the
Gizenga government in Stanleyville at the end of 1960
and the beginning of 1961, then in the Adoula governments in Leopoldville in 1961–1962 and 1963–1964; national deputy in 1965; arrested in July, 1967 and liberated
on November 23 of the same year.

Samalenge, Lucas   National Deputy of the Conakat in 1960; Under-Secretary of State for Information in Katanga during secession; died in November, 1961, in a hunting accident (according to the official version) or by assassination just as the UN published its report on the death of Lumumba.

Sapwe, Pius   Chief of police in Katanga during secession and Inspector General of the police in East Katanga beginning in 1963 and of the national police beginning in 1966.

Sendwe, Jason   President and National Deputy in 1960 of the Balubakat–Fedeka–Atcar cartel in Katanga; Vice-Prime Minister of the Adoula government of reconciliation in August, 1961; president of North Katanga in September, 1963; assassinated in Albertville in June, 1964.

Songolo, Alphonse   Elected National Deputy from the MNC–Lumumba and Minister of Communications in the first Congolese government in June, 1960; broke with Lumumba and was arrested by the Gizengist authorities, having been accused of secessionist attempts; very badly treated before being executed in February, 1961, in Stanlyville.

Tshisekedi, Etienne   Doctor of Law degree from Lovanium University; Assistant Commissioner for Justice in September, 1960; Minister of South Kasai; General Director of the École Nationale de Droit et d'Administration (ENDA, National School for Law and Administration); National Deputy from Panaco party in 1965;

Minister of the Interior and of Customs in the Mulamba government; then Minister of Justice from August to March, 1969; Minister of State in charge of Surveying, Scientific Research, and Management of Territory from March to August, 1969; ambassador to Rabat since August, 1969.

Tshombe, Moise   President of the Conakat; elected Provincial Deputy to Elizabethville in May, 1960; President of the Province, then of the State (in secession) of Katanga from 1960 to January, 1963; in exile in Europe (notably in Spain) from June, 1963, to June, 1964; head of the Congolese government from July, 1964, to October, 1965; President of the Conaco; elected National Deputy from the Conaco party in 1965; dismissed from this function in 1966; in exile in Madrid; condemned to death for high treason by a high court in Kinshasa on March 13, 1967; kidnapped by air over the Mediterranean June 30, 1967 and put under house arrest in Algeria, where he died on June 30, 1969.

Weregemere, Jean-Chrysostome   Elected Deputy from the Cerea party in 1960; Minister of Information in the central government of Stanleyville in 1961; Minister of the Adoula government in August, 1961; dismissed by a vote of censure by the Chamber on December 7, 1962; resident minister in Stanleyville in June, 1964; in Leopoldville since 1966.

Yumbu, Gabriel   Deputy from the PSA at the end of June, 1960; Minister of Finance in the Lumumbist government in Stanleyville at the end of 1960; spokesman for the PSA–Gizenga in opposition to Adoula in

1962–63; arrested in Leopoldville in September, 1963; joined the Conseil National de Liberation (CNL, National Council of Liberation) in Brazzaville. Since April, 1965, he has been Secretary General of the Conseil Suprème de la Révolution (CRS, Supreme Council of Revolution).

Index